The Business of Writing

Part 4 Independent Publishing

ELIZABETH DUCIE

Chudleigh Phoenix Publications

I began writing this book in Greece in 2018 and completed it in the same location one year later. To Roula and George and your staff at the wonderful Porto Kea Suites: you made working such a pleasure.

Most of all, to Michael; without you there would have been no Heathside and, therefore, no business books.

Contents

vi

Abbreviations

Abooks   Audio books

ALLi   Alliance of Independent Authors

ASIN   Amazon Standard Information Number

B&N   Barnes & Noble

BISAC   Book Industry Standards and Communications

CDs   Compact Discs

D2D   Draft2Digital

DIY   Do It Yourself

DRM   Digital Rights Management

Ebooks   Electronic books

Epub   Electronic publication

GDPR   General Data Protection Regulation

GIR   *Gorgito's Ice Rink*

Html   Hypertext markup language

IBAN   International Bank Account Number

IS   IngramSpark

ISBN   International Standard Book Number

KDP   Kindle Direct Print

MBA   Masters in Business Administration

NaNoWriMo	National Novel Writing Month
Q&A	Question and Answer
Pbooks	Physical books/paper books
PDF	Portable document format
POD	Print On Demand
Probus	Professional and Business Club
PUI	PublishDrive Unique Identifier
RAMM	Royal Albert Memorial Museum, Exeter
RTF	Rich Text Format
SPF	Self-Publishing Formula
SWIFT	Society for Worldwide Interbank Financial Telecommunication
U3A	University of the Third Age
UK	United Kingdom
USA/US	United States of America
USB	Universal Serial Bus
VAT	Value Added Tax
WI	Women's Institute
SWWJ	Society of Women Writers and Journalists
U3A	University of the Third Age
UK	United Kingdom of Great Britain and N. Ireland

USA	United States of America
VAT	Value Added Tax
VAT MOSS	VAT Mini One Stop Shop
WI	Women's Institute
Womags	Women's Magazines

Introduction

This is the fourth in my series of books on *The Business of Writing*. I've been writing technically for most of my working life. I've been writing creatively since 2005 and I've been working as a full-time writer since 2012.

However, I am also a small business owner—and have been since 1992. In the first year of our operation, we made more profit than a well-known computer manufacturer. (Okay, so that was the year that company made a loss—but you must admit it sounds impressive!) I have taught myself, through trial and error, to set up and run systems that work. Occasionally, I use the services of other individuals or organisations. In fact, knowing when to use a professional approach rather than DIY is an important skill in running a small business. But mostly I've done it myself.

I studied Business Administration at Cranfield School of Management and graduated with an MBA. I'm a scientist by education and training. I enjoy maths, project planning and system management. But most writers I meet are the complete opposite. They are horrified at the thought of having to stop creating to do the paperwork, the administration, and the 'boring bits' of running a business.

The Business of Writing is a toolbox of business skills for writers. My aim is to provide a simple route by which writers can set up and run their own small businesses. I want to identify the 'basic minimum standards' that must be achieved, while freeing you to spend the maximum possible time doing what you really want to be doing—writing.

I am neither an accountant nor a lawyer. I am simply a business owner with more than twenty-five years' experience. There will be times when taking the advice of another business practitioner is not enough. At those times, you need to consult the appropriate professional. I will keep reminding you of that throughout the book.

Throughout the series, I identify the questions you need to ask, rather than providing the answers (since they will often vary with individual circumstances).

My business is based in the United Kingdom, although I have worked all over the world and seen a variety of business systems in operation. Hence, inevitably, my knowledge of business systems tends to be biased towards there. The first edition of this series was very much UK-focused. The second editions of books 1-3 have been expanded to bring in a wider focus, particularly the United States. This part, dealing as it does with publishing principles, is applicable internationally. It is intended to be useful to all writers who are small business owners, wherever they may be located.

The series currently consists of four parts: *Part 1 Business Start-Up*; *Part 2 Finance Matters*; *Part 3 Improving Effectiveness*; and *Part 4 Independent Publishing*. Each part can be purchased individually as an ebook from a wide range of platforms. However, many people prefer their reference books in physical form and a composite volume of parts 1-3 is available for order as a Print on Demand (POD) paperback, as is part 4. A workbook associated with parts 1-3 is also available, in paperback format only.

If you purchased a copy of parts 1, 2 or 3 in the past and would like an updated version, drop me a line at elizabeth@elizabethducie.co.uk, with proof of original purchase, and I will send you an updated copy free of charge.

Section 1: The Basics

1. Getting Started

Writing a book is not easy, no matter what anyone tells you. You know those people who say: "I've always wanted to write a book"; or "I'm going to write a book one of these days"; or "I'd write a book if I had the time"? They all seem to think it's just a case of sitting down and putting words on paper.

Anyone who has actually written a book, or is in the process of doing so, knows it's not that easy. And there's a reason why, despite the saying "everyone has a book in them" not everyone ends up writing it. There's the research; the planning; the jotting down of random thoughts that occur on the bus or in the shower; the getting to know the characters; the first draft; the rewrites; the scrapping of several chapters; or even the starting again. I could go on. But anyone reading this has already gone through, or is going through, that process and knows exactly what I'm talking about.

But you know what? Compared to what comes next, writing the thing is something of a walk in the park. Getting it turned into a proper book, getting it noticed among the millions of other books fighting for readers' attention, and then getting those readers who do notice it to buy or borrow it, is a totally different ball game. It requires you to ask yourself a whole new set of questions; to take a series of new decisions; and to acquire a new set of business skills and tools. Which is what this book is about.

The first question you need to ask yourself is: which publishing route do you want to take? Given the title of this book, it's not difficult to work out which one we're mainly going to be talking about, but we're going to start by thinking about all the options.

2. What Does Publishing Involve?

There are all sorts of ways of defining the route to publication. The one I use is as follows:

- Writing

- Editing/Proofreading

- Production

- Marketing/Promotion

- Sales and Distribution

And it doesn't matter which publishing route you take. For a good quality book—and why would you settle for anything less?—all these stages need to be worked through. The main differences relate to who is responsible for, and who pays for, each one of them, apart from the first stage—the writing of the book. That's always down to you.

.

3 Traditional Publishing

The traditional route involves finding a publishing house which will take on your manuscript and publish it for you. The publishing house will be responsible for putting together a team with the skills to work through all the stages. You will work with the team on each stage.

Editing and proofreading will be done by professionals either from within the publishing house or subcontracted by them. The feedback and requested or suggested changes will come back to you, and you will be responsible for carrying them out. There will usually be a deadline by which you will be expected to complete them.

Production covers a whole range of activities, which we will look at in a later chapter. This is a stage in which you are not heavily involved. It's possible you will be consulted on such issues as cover design and pricing, but it's not mandatory; the publishing house will certainly make the final decisions.

Increasingly, the role of the author within the marketing/promotion stage will be a major one, at a time when marketing budgets are being slashed. You will often be expected to demonstrate you have an established platform before you are taken on, especially for a debut novel. You'll be required to keep a high profile on social media, and will be expected to make public appearances, especially during the immediate post-launch period.

Sales and distribution will be primarily the responsibility of the publishing house which will organise physical production of hardbacks, paperbacks and/or audio books. They will arrange for books to be stocked in libraries and bookshops. They will deal with all aspects of wholesaling and retailing.

From the point of view of financing, the publishing house will be responsible for all the costs. But on the other hand, they will retain most of the profit too. Under the traditional publishing model, the author is paid a percentage of the retail price; typically, this might be as low as 8%. Hence for a paperback selling in the UK at £6.99, the author would receive 56p; if the book is on sale in the supermarket for £3.99, then the royalties falls to 32p. Looking at the US market, a mass market paperback will be typically $9.99, from which the author would get 78cents.

Royalties tend to be paid once or twice per year, often three months after the end of a period. So, in the case of an annual payment system, for a book launched in January 2019, you might receive your first royalty statement and payment in March or April 2020.

Some authors receive advance payments on their royalties, which may be paid on signing the contract, on delivery of the manuscript, on publication—or a combination of these. The size of the advance, or whether one is paid at all, will depend on a number of factors including the popularity of the author, the potential market for the book, or the policy of the publisher. It's important to remember that this is an advance against future royalties, not an additional payment. So, no further royalties will be paid until the advance has been 'earned out'. For example, if you have an advance of $1,000 and you earn 78cents per book; you will have to reach sales of 1,283 before your advance is recovered; you would start earning additional royalties from the sale of copy number 1,284 onwards. However, on the other hand, if the book doesn't sell sufficient copies to earn out, there is no requirement for the advance to be repaid.

4. Independent Publishing

Increasingly, the independent publishing route is being seen as a viable alternative to traditional publishing. DIY publishing has been around for a long time. Back in the eighteenth century, Laurence Sterne self-published *Tristram Shandy*. In 1914, Virginia Woolf used her own imprint to publish her final novel, *Between the Acts*, and there have been many well-known authors between those dates who went down the same route.

But technology changes in the past decade or so have brought a whole new world into being: digital books. The platforms now exist for anyone who wishes to bring out their own books. And although many people think indie publishing is synonymous with digital printing, it can be used to produce not only ebooks, but also audio books (abooks) or physical books (pbooks). We will look at options for each of these in later chapters.

Before we look at the different options for independent publishing, I want to deal with one point up front because, as anyone who knows me will be aware, it's my biggest gripe with the industry today. Going down the independent publishing route is NOT taking the easy option. It is NOT the option of last resort. It is as difficult as, or even more difficult than, taking the traditional route. And therefore, it's a choice that should be taken as any business decision: after due consideration of the facts and weighing up of the pros and cons.

I saw a wonderful quote recently by author Greg White. "Five years ago, self-publishing was a scar," he said in a Bloomberg article. "Now it's a tattoo." It really struck a chord with me. After many years as the author of traditionally published textbooks, I began writing creatively and launched my first independently published book in July 2011. It was a collection of short stories penned with a friend and fellow writer, Sharon Cook. At the time, we knew the chances of getting a publishing deal for such a book, especially by two unknown fiction writers without an agent, were minimal. We decided to do it ourselves.

We started with a paperback and then put out the ebook six months later. In November 2012, we brought out our second collection. We were new to the industry and we made lots of mistakes, some of which I will share with you in later chapters. But we were learning. And we were growing as the latest incarnation of independent publishing was growing. But the thing I remember most from those days was the number of times we apologised for the fact we'd gone down the indie route. And the pitying looks we got from so many people when they heard what we'd done.

But times change. Indie Publishing 2.0 has been around for some time, and the early adopters are already talking about Indie Publishing 3.0. That's a whole different topic and I'm not planning on addressing it in this book, although you can find the definition of each term in the glossary. The point is, the traditional route is no longer the only way to gain respect and validation in this industry. And it certainly isn't necessarily the way to get the best financial deal.

5. The Best Thing…

The past ten or so years have been the most exciting in the publishing industry for a long time, and it looks like this trend is going to continue. Technological developments have made it possible for books to be written, produced and distributed much more easily than before. And not just physical books. The digital revolution has led to the invention of a whole new industry around ebooks and latterly audio books, which can be accessed on devices across the board, not just dedicated ereaders but everything from laptops and tablets to phone and watches.

Coupled with this has been the establishment of user-friendly platforms, some free at the point of use, some chargeable, which enable the author to do as much or as little as they wish themselves.

Inevitably, some users have been early adopters, diving straight in, making mistakes and learning as they go along. Others take a more cautious approach. And some find the whole thing, frankly, terrifying and just want someone to hold their hands and walk them through the process. And this has led to the third aspect to be considered. There's any amount of advice and support available out there. It's just necessary to decide which to use, which suggestions to follow, and how much to pay for the advice.

So, the best thing about the development of independent publishing over the past ten years is that anyone can publish anything and get it 'out there'.

6. The Worst Thing…

There was quite a backlash against independent publishing in the early years. Some of this is the unjustified (albeit quite understandable) reaction from the traditional arm of the industry to the brash newcomer threatening to take away its monopoly. But some of it is due to the fact that frankly, there is a lot of dross out there.

Some of you, knowing how supportive I am of indie publishing, might be shocked to hear me say that. But you're business people and to be successful, you need to be realistic and not fool yourselves. Not everything that's published is of the requisite quality. I'm sure you've downloaded at least one book in the past, either because it was free and looked like a good read, or because it was written by a friend and you're trying to be supportive, or because it had a great advertising campaign that caught your eye. Whatever the reason, you download the book, you eagerly turn to the opening chapter and what do you find? Badly written, poorly edited ramblings with two-dimensional characters, an excess of adverbs, and many spelling mistakes. You may plough on, trying to give the author the benefit of the doubt, but in most cases, you don't make it past chapter three.

A book like this should never have been published. It may well be the best story idea in the world, but if it's unreadable, no-one's going to be able to finish it. And the author has ruined their reputation before they start.

And from the point of view of your businesses, you run the risk of being tarred with the same brush. Or do you? If you ask the average reader, if such an individual exists, about the book they are currently reading, they will probably tell you they have no idea who published it; and frankly they don't care how a book is published, so long as it's a good book. However, there are literary festivals and competitions that still refuse to consider indie authors; and it's rare to see an independently published book reviewed in the mainstream media. Indies are starting to break into some of the major book award shortlists, and you can now join such organisations as The Society of Authors or the Romantic Novelists' Association; but it's slow progress. And every time a poor book is published, it prolongs this effect. Which is bad for business.

So, to recap, with the technology, the platforms and the support, the best thing about the development of independent publishing over the past ten years is that anyone can publish anything and get it 'out there'. The worst thing is that some people do so, even when they shouldn't.

7. Responsibility

The author as publisher (or authorpreneur as some people are calling it) has responsibility for ensuring all aspects of the publishing process are carried out professionally. But that doesn't mean they have to do everything themselves. It depends on their skills and preferences.

For example, I don't have an artistic bone in my body. I would never design my covers myself. Actually, that's not completely true. I designed the cover for Sunshine and Sausages myself. But that's only a bit of fun or, from a business point of view, my 'apprentice piece.' It's what I use to try out every new piece of technology that comes along.

For this series of non-fiction books on *The Business of Writing*, I used a template from Canva, which makes it a halfway house. It's an off-the-shelf design which I have customised, but it's been produced by a professional designer.

When it comes to my fiction, I wouldn't dream of doing anything other than engaging a professional cover designer. It's a cliché but true nevertheless that first impressions are critical and books are indeed judged by their cover. And whether it's a quest novel, a thriller or a romance, I want my potential readers to pick up the signals straight away. And for that, the cover needs to be professionally designed.

By the same token, I always engage a professional proofreader. I have a writing buddy with whom I work on the structural edit; I do line edits myself as my attention to detail is good and I have spreadsheets recording all aspects of the characters' back stories.

And I use a team of beta readers to give me detailed feedback before I do my final edits. But it's not physically possible to successfully proofread your own work. Your brain knows what should be there and sees that, whether it's written on the page or not.

Every writer is going to be different. There will be some skills you have, which you can satisfactorily employ. There will be other skills you lack completely and that's where you need to engage a professional.

But to reiterate the point with which I started this chapter: whoever carries out a particular activity, the responsibility for ensuring that it's carried out successfully rests with the publisher, and in the case of an indie, that's you.

8. Control

8.1 Introduction

One of the great things about being an indie publisher is the level of control you can retain over every detail of the process. To start with, you define the publishing budget. It can be a major investment if you decide to go down the route of producing paperbacks for stock—involving upfront printing costs and storage space. On the other hand, it can be done for no investment at all if you decide to go purely down the ebook route and can do all the formatting yourself. There are sound reasons for choosing either of these routes, or indeed anything in between, and we will look at that aspect in more detail in a later chapter.

8.2 Timing

There is a major advantage in being able to control timing—and thus greatly reducing timescales. When a book is going down the traditional route, it's competing for resources with all the other books in the publisher's portfolio. Depending on the size of that portfolio and the size of the publishing company, it can be anything from weeks to more than a year from the point of manuscript delivery to publication date. And since payment of royalties is made six months to one year in arrears, there can be quite a considerable time lag between finishing the book and seeing any money for it.

For indie authors however, timescales can be much shorter. When I brought out the paperback version of *The Business of Writing Parts 1-3*, I completed the final element of formatting on a Tuesday, just two weeks after I received the corrections from my proofreader and five weeks after I finished editing it. Within two days, I had copies in my hand from Amazon and three days later, the book was on sale at a writers' summer school. Money from face-to-face sales is available on the spot; and even royalty payments from Amazon are only sixty days in arrears.

Of course, one aspect of being in control is that you are able to slow down as well as speed up. When I set my objectives for 2017-8, I identified six non-fiction volumes and one novel, all due to be published within a four-month period. (Have I mentioned I believe in setting myself stretch targets?) Anyone with whom I shared those objectives tended to eye me pityingly before walking off, shaking their head. And of course, they were correct. It was an impossible timescale to set myself. Once I realised that, I knew I had to adjust my project plans, shortening some and lengthening the others. And because I am in control of my timescales, I was able to do just that.

8.3 Sales Channels

I've already mentioned that some authors decide to publish only in digital format, while others go just for paperbacks. And most authors these days fall somewhere in between. There are pros and cons to all approaches. As the master or mistress of your own destiny, you can pick and choose. And even change your mind as time goes on.

8.4 Marketing Campaigns

The old-fashioned way to market a book was to place adverts in newspapers and magazines, on television or, if you were really lucky, on posters in the Underground and on the sides of buses. And such physical marketing routes still exist, albeit with a huge price tag attached to them. At the other end of the spectrum, there are all the online opportunities for marketing: whether that's buying space on Amazon or Facebook; bidding for a slot on BookBub; or taking the free route by flooding the social media channels with posts. Most authors these days will construct a marketing strategy combining some or all of these options, depending on factors such as time, investment budget and preference. Once again, the point is the indie has the choice; you control which marketing channels you spend most time and money upon. The amount of marketing you have to do yourselves is not necessarily that different from that of the traditionally published author. But at least you do have control over what you do and when.

8.5 Pricing Strategy

A friend of mine decided to go down the route of independent publishing, using a full serviced package. She paid a huge price for the privilege—that's a different story—but found she wasn't in complete control of everything that happened. Actually, that's not quite true. She did have control; she just didn't always realise what decisions she had to make. And one of those was on pricing. Unlike those of us who go down the DIY route, she didn't have day-to-day access to sales data. And therefore, it was a while before she realised she wasn't selling ebooks at the rate she had hoped to. On checking her Amazon page, she found the ebook was on sale for a high price, closer to that of a paperback than a typical ebook. Once she'd seen this, she instructed the service company to reduce the price which they did, albeit reluctantly—and her sales started to climb.

The whole area of digital sales prices is one of constant discussion. Some people swear by the 'pile 'em high, sell them cheap' approach. Some believe making the first in a series available as 'perma-free'—giving it away all the time, rather than as a short-term promotion—is guaranteed to lead to sales of the other books in the series at full price, or at least for some money. Others believe authors should respect themselves and their work by charging a suitable price for it—thus cultivating fewer leads but more useful ones: readers who are willing to pay a fair price for a book and will go on to buy more if they like the author's work.

We'll have a look at this argument in more detail elsewhere in the book, but the point to emphasise at this moment is that as an indie author/publisher you are the one in control of the pricing strategy. You decide at what price to set it.

8.6 Quality Of The Finished Product

We've already looked at the fact that as an indie author, you have responsibility for making sure everything is done in as professional a manner as possible; and it goes without saying that the quality of the contents should be good. But there are also all sorts of options for the physical quality of the product. Is it a mass market book people are going to buy, read once and then give to the charity shop? If so, then producing it as a hardback with top-quality gloss finish, extra thick paper and coloured illustrations is probably not the way to go. On the other hand, if it's a volume of small but perfectly formed poems with associated illustrations, destined for the coffee tables of friends and family, then cut-price binding and low grade matt paper is not going to be appropriate. The point is, choices can be made, and they can be made by the person in charge of the budget and the project plan: you, the indie author.

8.7 Cover Design And Title

I have talked on occasion to traditionally published author friends who have had changes made to their title or have been forced to accept cover designs which they don't believe are representative of their book's content, because the publisher believes their choices will make for better sales within that particular genre. And in many cases, the publisher may be right, galling as that may be for the author. But as an indie, you make the choices, not someone else who probably has less emotional capital invested in the project. And some of those choices may be wrong, but that's okay as long as you learn from those mistakes.

9. *Caveat Emptor*

At this really exciting time in this industry's history, you have so many opportunities to evolve in the way that suits you best. But it's also a scary time. There are a lot of newbie authors trying to work out what they need to do; maybe looking for someone to hold their hand as they take their first baby steps.

And there are certainly plenty of people out there willing to hold out their hands to help you—at a price. There's an old saying—or if there isn't, there should be—that the only people who make money from a legal battle are the lawyers. And by the same token, it often seems the only people making money in the field of independent publishing are the service companies, consultants and gurus. Every time you turn around, there's someone else looking to take money off you in return for a sure-fire way of hitting the top of the charts.

Now I'm not saying all the service companies, consultants and gurus are charlatans. That would be silly—especially in a book that's part of a series of reference texts. There's lots of genuine support out there—some of it generously provided for free, some of it sold for a reasonable price. But there are also a lot of sharks. All I'm saying is think carefully before handing money over to anyone. Check the company or person out. Try to get word of mouth recommendations from people you trust within the industry. Make sure any contract you sign is a fair one. Being a member of an organisation like the Alliance of Independent Authors or the Society of Authors is a good place to start.

Not all advice is good advice. Cost is not always an indicator of quality. But on the other hand, if something looks too good to be true, then it very probably is.

10. Steps To Publication (1-3)

10.1 Introduction

There are all sorts of ways to describe this industry we are part of, and different ways of defining the steps you need to take to become a published author. And these steps have to be taken in one way or another irrespective of whether you are going down the traditional route, aiming for independent publishing—or anything in between. The next few chapters work through the model I use—and if you've got to choose a model to work with, then why not use this one—it's as good as any other.

10.2 Writing

Nothing can happen until that first draft is written. It will probably be a long way from the form in which it finally hits the bookshelves or ereaders, but it's the first step in the process. Get it done, and don't worry too much if it's rough around the edges. You can always edit rubbish; you can't edit a blank page.

10.3 Editing

Again, there are different ways of defining this one word: structural edit, copy edit, line edit, beta reading are just some of the ways in which this process is carried out. Some people only use one of the ways; others use all of them. Each time I edit a novel I give it a new version number. My debut novel, *Gorgito's Ice Rink*, was on version twenty-one by the time I finally published it—and it had taken nearly eight years to get that far. These days, I can finish a novel in around twelve to eighteen months, but even so, there are usually at least four different versions on file by publication day.

10.4 Proofreading

No matter how good you are at editing, you need a professional proofreader. It's the only way to eliminate all those little errors which your own eyes are tricked into missing by a brain that knows what's supposed to be written, and therefore sees that rather than what's really on the page.

Once these three stages have been completed, we have a manuscript that's ready for publication. This book is about independent publishing, not about how to write. So, we're going to start from the assumption that these three stages have been achieved successfully and move on to talk about the rest of the steps in more detail.

11. Step 4: Layout

Being an indie author means having the right to choose how you do things, and the independence to do things differently from the accepted way if you wish to. But as business people, you also want to sell your books. And I've never believed in reinventing the wheel just for the sake of it. If you can learn anything from the traditional route, and use it effectively in your own publishing, then you should take advantage of that. And one area where I believe this applies is in the layout, in particular with physical books.

Some years ago, I managed to talk my way into one of the larger literary festivals near me and even managed to get my book stocked in the on-site bookstore, run by a well-known high street chain. The guys setting up the bookstore picked up my novel and exclaimed, "wow, it looks like a proper book!"! (and that exclamation mark is deliberately duplicated, as my emotion is greater than his). Part of me was really insulted at the implication this was unusual in an independently published book; but part of me was also delighted to receive vindication of the approach I'd taken to cover design and chapter layout.

Before I start laying out a book I go to my bookshelves and pull out a volume from the same genre or type of book, by an author and or a publisher I trust—and these latter are usually members of the 'big five' traditional publishing houses—and look at what they do. Then I shamelessly copy this layout.

To date, I have always started with the layout for the physical book, since this is the most complex, with page numbers, blank pages to ensure correct orientation (left-hand page versus right-hand page), and differing margins for spine and outer sides of the page. Once I've got that sorted, I make a copy of the master file and strip out the formatting to make it suitable for an ebook. And when you get to that part, there are a variety of ways to proceed, depending on which platforms you are using and how technically proficient you are.

Even though I use books off my shelf to guide me towards the final look of the book, there are a number of shortcuts you can use. Both KDP and IngramSpark provide templates; you can also set them up via software such as Scrivener; or you can use a dedicated programme like Vellum (for Mac users) or Calibre (for Windows users). In any event, it's not necessary to start from scratch each time.

I set up my main template when I published my first novel back in 2014. These days, I make a copy of the master file from the previous book and cut and paste the new material over the top. I know that's a little long-winded and there are faster, more automated methods, but it works well for me and, as the saying goes, 'if it ain't broke, don't fix it.' But, a word of caution if you are going to take this approach. Make sure you do a final read through of the finished file, to ensure there are none of the chapters remaining from the earlier book. An easy mistake to make, especially if the new book has fewer chapters than the previous one, but one that will confuse the hell out of your readers.

And while we're talking about layout, a reiteration of earlier points about your cover design. It needs to be professional and appropriate for your book. If you're writing romantic comedy, then pastel colours, swirly writing and even a bit of glitter is what your readers will expect. But if it's a deep psychological thriller or a fantasy with death and destruction, then your readers will be looking for something much darker. A professional cover designer will understand this and will guide you in the right direction.

When I brought out my first three books, all collections of short stories, I used a local artist to design my covers. His illustrations were wonderful and fitted our purpose perfectly. So, when I prepared to publish my first novel, I asked him to come up with some ideas. The book was based in Russia and featured a skater and an eponymous hero. My friend produced a beautiful illustration featuring all three aspects, which I still display when I give talks on that book. But as a cover, it didn't work. And I couldn't decide what was wrong. It was my sister who put her finger on it: "It looks like a children's book," she said. And she was right. Neither my friend nor I had the experience to design a cover appropriate for an adult quest novel. I went out and found a professional designer who did have the appropriate experience— and the rest is history.

12. Step 5: Publication

12.1 Introduction

This is the stage at which you start deciding which format(s) you want your book to appear in. So, let's begin with the traditional format.

12.2 The Physical Book.

There are two options for a physical book: the hardback version and the paperback. These days, the latter is by far the more common choice for readers due to a number of factors including size, weight and cost. Hardback books are less common, certainly for indie publishers; and even for many traditionally published authors, the paperback option is available right from launch day. There are some publishers who continue to follow the traditional route of publishing the hardback initially and then following it up six to twelve months later with a paperback, but this is becoming less common.

Whichever format you decide on, there are two main options for production. The traditional way was always to organise a print run from a printer. This is still an option but has implications for both investment, since the costs must be paid upfront, and for storage. It also means there are two transactions in the sales process: between the publisher and the printer; and between the reader and the publisher. Indie publishers who go down this route will tend to find a local printer and order a relatively short run, balancing quantity against unit cost: the larger the print run, the lower the unit cost, but the greater the upfront payment to be made. The benefits of this approach include having stock available at short notice if a selling opportunity arises; and having the flexibility to reduce prices or offer discounts for bulk purchases if appropriate. The disadvantages include cost and the possibility of being left with unsold copies.

The more modern approach, and one taken by many, if not most, indie publishers, is to use the technology of Print on Demand (or POD). In this case, the minimum batch size is one copy. It's possible for orders to be placed directly by the reader, so the transaction is between the printer and the reader, with no involvement of the publisher in between. Postage is paid by whoever places the order, so again, this can be directly between reader and printer. The main disadvantages of this approach are there is less flexibility in terms of having stock available— although with a turnaround of less than twenty-four hours in some cases, this may not be a major issue— and that the unit cost is higher. Hence there is less flexibility for offering your readers discounts with this printing option.

There are a number of platforms for producing POD books. The popular one for many people in recent years was CreateSpace, Amazon's original platform.

However, Amazon phased out this platform in 2018, replacing it with a paperback option from Kindle Direct Publishing (KDP).

Another alternative is to use IngramSpark, the indie arm of Ingram Content Group, the world's largest wholesaler of print and electronic books. The set-up is a little more complex and there are charges associated both with raising a new title and initiating any changes, but the distribution channels are much wider. Charges can be reduced or even eliminated by using discount codes available for example to members of ALLi (Alliance of Independent Authors) or participants in NaNoWriMo (National Novel Writing Month). Additionally, libraries and bookshops are happier to deal with IngramSpark than with Amazon.

One step further in the production of physical books would be to consider large print versions for those with visual impairment. These are less popular than they used to be, since it is possible to adjust the size of the font on ereaders, but it's still an option. Most people will tend to do this through a specific publishing company that specialises in this format.

12.3 Ebooks

There are a variety of platforms that can be used to publish ebooks: direct to Amazon and nowhere else; via an aggregator like Draft2Digital, PublishDrive or Smashwords; direct to the other main channels, such as Apple iBooks, Kobo, and Barnes & Noble; or a combination approach. We will look at this in much more detail later in the book.

12.4 Abooks

Audio books have been around for a good while. But they are a relatively new option for indie publishers. Once again, changes in technology have brought opportunities within our grasp. Production of an abook is an expensive process, but there are options to help spread the upfront cost. And from a technology point of view, there's the possibility of bypassing physical media altogether—we used to buy a lot of 'talking books' on cassette tape for the car,

but these days they are all on CDs or a USB stick—
and going straight to download mode.

13. Step 6: Marketing

13.1 Introduction

Once again, there are all sorts of ways of thinking about marketing. I tend to think about it in three phases.

- Pre-launch

- Launch

- Ongoing

Let's have a look at each one in turn.

13.2 Pre-launch

The pre-launch period can be between six and twelve months and is the time to raise expectations. This might be by cover reveals; a diary charting progress through the writing/editing process; or other activities aimed at piquing readers' interests. This is relatively easy for traditionally published authors where timescales are quite long anyway. One of the benefits of indie publishing is its speed and flexibility. Many independently published authors bring out more than one book in a year and therefore having a long pre-launch period may not be possible.

13.3 Launch

This is the time for making a big noise, trying to attract everyone's attention. So long as it doesn't happen too often and so long as you don't go completely over the top, readers will tend to forgive you jumping up and down and metaphorically saying, "buy my book, buy my book" even though perceived wisdom says this shouldn't be regular practice on social media.

This is the time for launch parties, whether they're physical face-to face-affairs or virtual ones online. I tend to do both but need to plan my time carefully. Lessons I've learned over the past few years include: do not try to run a virtual launch and a physical launch on the same day—it's just too exhausting; and by the same token, trying to keep an online party going for twelve hours is a little overambitious as well.

In addition to the parties, you need to keep a regular presence in the various social media platforms you use. But as I mentioned above, simply saying, "buy my book, buy my book" will tend to turn off potential readers rather than inspiring them to hit the 'buy now' button.

The trick with social media is to make friends; it's human nature to want to support friends and, despite the wishes of Amazon it's a fact that, at least initially, many of the people who buy your books are people you 'know' online, whether that's via Facebook, Twitter, Instagram or other such platforms. Use these platforms to chat to people; engage them in conversations; ask questions that will trigger discussions. My novels are set in locations other than the UK; I devise a month-long campaign where I post pictures relating to the setting of the book or incidents that take place within the story. I start by posting every couple of days and gradually ramp it up to daily posts in the last two weeks before the launch.

This is also a good time to raise the interest level in the local press, either by press releases or direct contact. Having contacts in the local media is an important tool in your box. Also look out for opportunities for appearances on local radio. If you can get onto or into the national or international media, so much the better. But the tagline of 'local author' is often a strong one, especially if your book has a local link. Although my novels are all set outside the UK, I tend to give my main characters homes, or at least second homes, in Devon, hoping to attract readers who wish to find an association with their own community.

The blog tour is a popular promotional tool during the launch period, although there is some disagreement about whether it actually increases sales of the book. What it does do is raise awareness of the book, as tens of bloggers, many with large readerships and followings, read, review, publish articles about, share, retweet etc. about the book. In the past, I've always organised my own blog tours, by calling in favours from writer friends. But for a relatively small fee, it's possible to get a tour organised for you. I used one of these for my last novel and was delighted with the outcome.

13.4 Ongoing

After the excitement of the launch has died down, it's not possible to sit back on your laurels and watch the sales continue to roll in. It's a hugely crowded marketplace out there and unless you can manage to keep the promotion going and remind people of your book's presence, it will simply vanish without trace, buried under a huge pile of other books brought out after yours. So there needs to be a strategy for promoting your brand as well as your individual books on an ongoing basis.

This is a really brief overview of the topic of marketing, since it is not the main focus of this book. There are plenty of other resources out there dealing with it. I would particularly recommend anything on the subject by Joanna Penn of The Creative Penn; the podcasts and training courses from Mark Dawson of Self-Publishing Formula (SPF); and the guides published by the Alliance of Independent Authors (ALLi).

14. Step 7: Sales And Distribution

14.1 Introduction

Having produced the book and promoted it to death, it's necessary to consider the ways in which you will get copies into your readers' hands, via your sales and distribution channels. I'm going to start with traditional, physical copies and look at the options here; then move on to the newer options of ebooks and abooks.

14.2 Face-To-Face Sales

This is certainly one of the more satisfying ways of selling a book. Seeing your work in someone else's hands, especially someone who has read your work before and tells you how they are looking forward to reading the new story, is one of the most pleasing parts of being an author. And for this reason, face-to-face-sales is my favourite distribution channel.

It might be via a launch party—with the right guest list, this is the opportunity to sells tens of copies in one go. It might be via a bookstall at a meeting of the Women's Institute (WI), the University of the 3rd Age (U3A), or similar organisation which puts on monthly events and is always looking for speakers. These events can be mixed in terms of sales: I've spoken at some where I've sold fifteen copies; while at others, not one book has been bought. You need to be philosophical about it. But on the other hand, these organisations usually pay a fee to speakers, so it's rare to come away completely empty-handed.

It might be via a stall at a book fair or literary festival; or at a more general craft fair. The advantage of the former is that everyone walking past your stall is likely to be a reader of some kind; but the disadvantage is there will be lots of competition for their money. With the latter type of event, there's less competition, as bookstalls are rare—apart from second-hand stalls which are often run for charity—but on the other hand, the people walking past will be a mixture of readers and non-readers.

And don't underestimate the opportunity presented by friends and family who've already bought and read your books. If they've enjoyed them—and why wouldn't they—then encourage them to think of books when they're writing their Christmas present lists or planning a birthday treat. There are all sorts of opportunities for repeat sales; you just have to look out for them and take advantage of them whenever you can.

14.3 Bookstores

For an independently published author, it is harder to get books stocked in bookstores. But it's by no means impossible. It just takes some careful planning (and sometimes, a lot of begging). It also takes a professional, business-like approach. If you just turn up unannounced during a busy time of the day and try to persuade a member of staff to stock your books, you will make yourself look unprofessional and are highly unlikely to be successful. You need to take off your author's hat and put on your publisher's one.

Take the time and trouble to find out the name of the person you need to speak to; make an appointment in advance; arrive on time, dressed appropriately; and with suitable printed material to provide the required information. It's useful to produce an information sheet in the same format as the ones produced by the traditional publishers. The bookseller will be used to receiving information in this format and may be more receptive as a result. You will also need to be prepared to either accept or negotiate a rate of commission acceptable to the bookstore while, hopefully, still allowing you to make a profit—or at the very least, to break even if it is primarily an exercise in increasing visibility.

Let's start with the smaller, independent bookstores. They're often happy to feature books by local authors and will also sometimes host book launches or signing sessions. In this case, the approach needs to be made directly to the person within the store who's responsible for decision-making; this will often be the owner. There is often more room for negotiation on rates of commission in these shops as well. However, it's more usual for stock to be accepted on the basis of sale or return only. And independent bookstores are increasingly becoming rarer; not every town will have one.

On the other hand, there are the larger bookstores, like Waterstones and WHSmith in the UK or Barnes & Noble in the US. In the former, in particular, the strategy seems to vary over time and sometimes it's easier to get into a store than at others. It's important to contact the local store manager, and often the decision will depend on his/her attitude to local indie authors. But even with a supportive local manager, it will still be necessary to satisfy the requirements of the centralised systems. This means, in addition to a professionally designed cover and internal format, having your own ISBN which defines you as the publisher, as opposed to using a free one provided by the publishing platform. The larger chains will not stock books with a KDP ISBN because they see Amazon as a major rival.

For the same reason, it's necessary to have stock that can be sourced via a major distributor, whether you are supplying copies from your own back bedroom or sourcing via a POD system. As a publisher, I'm registered with both Gardners and Bertrams, the two main book wholesalers in the UK, used both by the major bookstores and by libraries. If an order is placed via either of them, I receive an email and can send the required quantity to them for onward distribution.

An even better method from the point of view of distribution is to use the POD service provided by IngramSpark. The set-up is a little more complex than with KDP, and there are associated charges; but these can often be alleviated via discount codes and once set-up has been worked through a couple of times, it becomes very straightforward.

The larger chains may consider buying copies for stock rather than taking them on a sale or return basis, so this provides another advantage for the author/publisher.

14.4 Other Retailers

We do not have an independent bookstore in our small town. However, I've found a number of other outlets willing to stock my books. The local Post Office has a stand which moves around the shop as displays are rearranged; sometimes it's hidden away in a corner, especially when seasonal stock is being featured, but sometimes it's front and centre, right where people are queuing and therefore with time to browse. And at times like that, sales tend to go up.

I've had stock featured in the gift shops associated with local tourist attractions. These are always full of people eager to spend money on a souvenir of their visit or a gift for friends and family. I suspect my sales would be better if I wrote thrillers based in the Haldon Hills rather than in Russia and Southern Africa, but nevertheless, there has been a steady trickle of sales over the years. Similarly, a local café had a display on their information table for a long time and sold quite a few copies as a result.

The single most successful outlet at one time was the petrol station just outside town on the main dual carriageway into Cornwall. Lots of holidaymakers stop there on their way westward, and I guess they're thinking of possible rainy days ahead, when they stock up on reading material.

But one thing to consider when deciding on where to offer your books for sale is the distance from home and therefore the cost of petrol to drive over and restock. If it's a busy outlet and sales are likely to be high, then it's worth going a bit further afield. But when I first started on this publishing journey, back in

2011, my co-author and I toured the county offering our books to shops all over the place. We ended up with ones and twos in Post Offices and gift shops over a twenty-mile radius. And with only tiny clientele and even smaller sales, it became financially non-viable to drive around restocking every so often. We ended up phoning periodically for an up-to-date stock check and emailing invoices for the occasional sales. In the end, I pulled all the stock back and concentrated on a few local outlets where it was more economic to visit.

14.5 Online Sales

These days, some authors make a positive decision to produce in the digital market only and NOT to produce physical books at all. And while I wouldn't go down that path myself—there are far too many readers around who will only read a 'proper book'—it's a decision I can understand. And some of those digital-only authors are making a very good living that way. But the reverse—producing only physical books and not making them available digitally—is not a sensible option. And with platforms available with no upfront charges, why would anyone want to go down that road?

There are dire warnings occasionally that the digital market is slowing down or is even in decline, but it's inconceivable it should die away altogether. And who knows what technology might come along in the next decade? After all, the first ereaders only went on sale in 2004. This is very much a young, but rapidly growing and evolving market.

And the first decision to make is whether to give exclusivity to Amazon or whether to go 'wide'. Exclusivity means your ebook is only available on the Amazon platform. And note, I said ebook. Your decisions in this area have no impact on your strategy for selling physical books or audio books. We will deal separately with those later.

14.6 Amazon Exclusivity

Amazon is the only ebook platform to offer an exclusivity package. There are a number of undoubted advantages in taking this option, which is done by enrolling in KDP Select. Firstly, it's currently the largest seller of ebooks in many countries, and certainly in the UK and the US. Far more people go straight to Amazon when looking for books (and many other things for that matter) than anywhere else.

Only having one platform means one master file, one location to deal with any changes or updates, one source of income to account for, and thus one set of administrative tasks.

Being exclusive with Amazon gives you access to specific marketing tools not available to non-exclusive authors or books. There is the possibility of offering the book for free, five days in every ninety. This can be done as a single block of five days; five individual days; or any combination thereof.

Or there is the possibility of running a countdown promotion, where the price is drastically reduced for a short period of time and then gradually counts back up to normal. For example, a book normally priced at

$3.99 might be on sale at $0.99 for one day, rising to $1.99 for one day, then to $2.99 for one day, before returning to full price. And throughout the time of the promotion, the royalty rate remains at that of the full price (70% instead of 35%). This promotion is only available to purchasers using the UK or US sites, at the present time.

Books enrolled in KDP Select are eligible for Kindle Unlimited, a subscription service available to readers in certain major territories; currently twelve are listed: France, Germany, Italy, Spain and UK in Europe; Brazil, Canada, Mexico and US in the Americas, plus Australia and Japan. This is a subscription service where readers can download as many books as they wish for a monthly fee. Payment to the author is based on pages read and while the rate appears minuscule and works out at a fraction of a cent per page, some authors have found this a good source of income.

A related scheme also available to books enrolled with KDP Select is the Kindle Owners Lending Library, a service currently available to Amazon Prime members in the UK, US, Germany, France and Japan. Payment in this scheme is also based on the number of pages read.

And finally, there is a possibility books enrolled within KDP Select are subject to preferential visibility measures from Amazon; measures such as inclusion in the daily deals promotions. However, no-one really understands the Amazon algorithm and if anyone does fathom it out, Amazon changes it! So, this is probably the least important of the benefits of being exclusive, and may well be apocryphal.

On the other hand, there are a number of disadvantages of being exclusive with Amazon. Firstly, enrolment is for a ninety-day period. Your ability to be flexible and change strategy is restricted. And re-enrolment is automatic, unless you remember to uncheck the box; if you miss the expiry date, your options are frozen for a further three months.

By definition, no book enrolled in KDP Select can be sold on any other platform, so you are restricted in terms of the advertising and promotion you can utilise.

Depending on your ambitions for your book, exclusivity might be completely the wrong strategy. For example, it is impossible to become a New York Times bestseller with an ebook enrolled in KDP Select.

Amazon does not allow books to be given away for free on a regular basis, or perma-free, as it is called. So the strategy, employed by some authors, of providing the first book in a series for free in order to encourage people to buy and read further volumes, is not one you could employ. Although there is a way around this prohibition for books published 'wide', as we will discuss later on.

And finally, there's the 'eggs in one basket' syndrome. Having your books enrolled in KDP Select means you are completely at the mercy of Amazon in terms of promotion, sales and distribution. Many people are concerned about the way Amazon changes rules, imposes restrictions and generally calls the shots. For some, this is an acceptable disadvantage when weighed against the benefits. But for others, the cost is too high. Without wishing to be a doom-monger, what happens if Amazon goes out of business? Where would that leave your books, your sales and your income? And to anyone who says: Amazon is so big; it's never going to fail, my answer is: that's probably what Barings Bank and Cambridge Analytica thought—but look how easily their fortunes turned around.

And don't forget this whole digital marketplace is less than twenty years old. Technology changes so rapidly none of us really knows what the next decade or so might bring.

It's important to mention here that this decision is made on a book-by-book basis. It is perfectly possible to have one or more of your books enrolled in KDP Select, while others are available across all the platforms. This allows you to define your strategy for each book or series individually. You will see in the Case Study chapter at the end of the book, that this is exactly the approach I have taken.

14.7 Going Wide

The alternative to granting exclusivity to Amazon is known as going wide. It means making your books available on some or all of the other platforms which facilitate sale and distribution of ebooks. In this field there are a handful of large players and a whole raft of smaller names. And if you're going down this road, there's really no reason not to go for every platform available. Even if sales numbers are relatively low, a sale is a sale, when all's said and done.

The major players are Apple, who sell ibooks; Kobo; and Barnes & Noble. Other include Scribd, Tolino, 24symbols, and Playster. There are also platforms dealing specifically with supplying libraries, such as Overdrive and Bibliotecha. The borrowing of ebooks via libraries is a relatively new departure, but it's an area likely to grow in the future.

At this point, there are even more decisions to be made. If you are going wide, you can either publish your book to one of the aggregator sites of which the main ones are Draft2Digital (D2D), Smashwords and rapidly-growing newcomer, Publish Drive. Or you can publish directly onto the individual sites. Or, and this is the more common approach, you can do a mixture of the two. I have been using D2D and Smashwords, since between them they gave me the widest possible reach; but I have recently started migrating some of my titles towards direct publishing on the main sites and staying with D2D and Smashwords for the remainder. Plus, I am also investigating Publish Drive which claims to have a wider geographical spread.

Before we look at the mechanics of each option, let's think about the pros and cons of going wide. And inevitably, they will tend to be the converse of the pros and cons already listed for staying exclusive.

Although Amazon is undoubtedly the largest player in the UK and US markets, it does not have the majority of the business in all countries, and its competitors are not all tiny. For example, Kobo is big in Canada, while Tolino is a major player in Germany. Over time, the dominance of Amazon will inevitably be chipped away at by the other companies.

There are no tie-in periods and therefore flexibility is increased. There are opportunities for promotion on some or all of the other platforms. Each has different approaches, and different strategies may be employed.

There is no restriction on pricing and perma-free is a permitted strategy (although, it is a question of debate as to whether this is still as good a strategy as it used to be). And this is the way you can get around the ban by Amazon on perma-free books. Amazon insists on being the lowest price retailer and will always at least match the sales prices of other suppliers. And this policy trumps the 'no perma-free' rule. Once your book is available for free on one or more other platforms, you simply email Amazon and point out it is selling your book at a more expensive level than someone else and will they please invoke price-matching; they will immediately—or sometimes slightly more slowly—reduce the price to zero.

And most important of all, you avoid the 'eggs in one basket' syndrome. If something goes wrong with one platform, there are plenty of others to concentrate on.

Of course, there are disadvantages to this approach, which once again will be the opposite of those described in relation to exclusivity.

Initially, sales will tend to be lower on the other platforms than on Amazon. Since the Free and Countdown tools are only available within KDP Select, you will not have access to these opportunities for promotion.

There will be an increased level of administration, depending on the number of platforms employed. And don't forget for those of you outside the US, there will be a need to register your tax information to avoid double taxation. If you don't get this part of the paperwork sorted out correctly, you might end up paying an extra 30% in taxation on the royalties coming from the US.

And each time you make a change to one of your books, you need to amend and reload a new file for each separate platform. This is certainly an encouragement of the 'right first time' principle.

14.8 Using An Aggregation Service

Once again, there are advantages and disadvantages to be considered before you decide whether to go for one or more of the aggregators. They are quicker and easier to use. They will take a single file, convert it to relevant formats and deliver it to a whole range of platforms. A single administrative process, one simple form, should also deal with the US double taxation threat as well.

On the other hand, using these sites increases the cost or, should I say, reduces the net royalties that you receive. They are more costly than going direct, but since their charge is only a small percentage of the purchase price, it may be considered as a price worth paying.

The first of these services, in terms of age, is Smashwords which was launched by Mark Coker in 2008. Being the oldest, it's slightly clunky to operate, and it is much less forgiving with regard to rogue formatting within the file, but there's a detailed manual, which can be downloaded for free and which provides step-by-step instructions. Also, the quality assurance features it runs mean all problems have to be sorted out before the book goes live. So, although it might be a pain initially, there is a better chance of getting a satisfactorily formatted book by the time it goes live. The other advantage of Smashwords is that as it's been around longer, it delivers to more markets than D2D.

And as an aside, Mark Coker, the founder of Smashwords, does a huge amount of data analysis and periodically publishes presentations full of interesting information about what is working currently within the marketplace; what no longer works; and what you need to think about moving forward.

A more modern and easier piece of software comes from D2D. This works in the same way as Smashwords but has a more user-friendly website. However, its range of final platforms is currently smaller than Smashwords. In recent years, I have used both services, choosing D2D for my main one and then selecting additional platforms to service via Smashwords. Of the two, D2D is the simpler, as will be seen in a later chapter when we look at the technical aspects. It is flexible and quick to use; it provides downloadable files in each of the main formats, and there are no restrictions on what you may do with those files. In fact I have been known, in the past, to use D2D to set up the files for downloading, even when I intend to provide exclusivity to Amazon and will not be launching on the wider platforms at all.

14.9 Direct To Platforms

The final option for 'going wide', and the most DIY one, is to go direct to the individual platforms. This is the most cost effective option, as there is only one commission to pay in each case, but administratively it's more complex. It increases the number of files you have to maintain; it increases the number of customers paying you; and it increases the number of potentially different systems you have to learn. It does, however, offer additional benefits in terms of promotional opportunities.

The recommendation of organisations such as the Alliance of Independent Authors (ALLi) and individual authors that have already gone down this road, is that it's worth doing it for the majors: Apple iBooks, Kobo, and Barnes & Noble, but that for the smaller ones, it's better to go with an aggregation service.

14.10 Direct Sales

Of course, there is one further option, which is to sell your ebooks directly to your readers, as many of us currently do with our paperbacks. This is an approach which is less common at the moment but is a major plank in the strategy of some of the early adopters of technology, who are looking at so-called Self-publishing 3.0, the next phase in the business of being an authorpreneur.

To sell your ebooks yourself, you need a place from which to sell, which would generally be a specialised website set up as an electronic store. It can be done reasonably easily with some of the standard website providers such as WordPress. But it needs an element of technological expertise. And it needs to be maintained, which takes time. Do you really need to add this task to all the others on your To Do list?

Then you need a method of delivery, based on the required file format. This would probably be a service like BookFunnel. And you need a method of collecting payment. This would be via an electronic bank such as PayPal.

You would also need to consider how you would approach and find your readers. With the major platforms you are halfway there, as the only people who visit those sites will be readers looking for books to buy; in other words, warm leads. But how are you going to persuade those potential buyers to visit your own little website, or even to find it if they have never heard of you? Facebook ads would still be open to you, but those operated by Amazon and BookBub would not; the former for obvious reasons and the latter because they only have buttons for the major platforms at the moment. There would be an even greater than normal need for a high level of promotion on the various social media channels.

And finally, there is the thorny issue of Value Added Tax (VAT) in Europe. On 1st January 2015, the European Union, in their wisdom, changed the rules for digital sales, a category into which ebooks fall. Unlike physical books, which are exempt from VAT, ebooks are charged at the national rate (which varies across the various member states). To make things even worse, the point of sale for digital goods and services is judged to be at the buyer's place, rather than the seller's. And to make things absolutely terrible, there is no lower limit below which VAT registration is not required, whereas, for example in the UK, a sole trader or business with non-digital sales of—currently—£80,000 does not have to register for, or charge VAT. This means anyone making direct sales of ebooks to the customer has to be registered for VAT and has to make quarterly returns based on sales in each of the different countries.

This whole topic is a contentious one; and it is likely that the rules will be amended at some point to make it less onerous for small businesses. And it is actually possible to use a digital sales platform which will deal with VAT collection and returns for you. But the responsibility for getting it right will still remain with you. Professional advice is definitely recommended if you decide to go down this route.

15. Summarising

Before we move on to the specific technical aspects of being an independent publisher, let's just recap on the principles of the situation. First and foremost, as both author and publisher, you are the Creative Director of your project. You have the final say in every aspect and are responsible for every stage, although that does not mean you have to carry out every activity yourself; in fact, it's rare for any one person to be able to do everything themselves. But when you contract other people to do things for you, you are the client, you are paying the bill and you are calling all the shots.

Being an indie means being able to greatly reduce the timescales and to be much more flexible. It's perfectly possible to successfully launch a new product, i.e. a book, in a matter of weeks or months. But on the other hand, the window of opportunity for taking advantage of that new product is as long as you wish it to be. It's perfectly possible to leave your major marketing push until you have developed your portfolio; and then starting on the sales and marketing in earnest. In fact, that's the approach I've taken. I've spent the last three years writing and publishing a series of thrillers. I've done a certain amount of marketing around launch times, but on an ongoing basis, I've allowed the writing to take centre stage. With the launch of book three, I have now moved into a major marketing phase.

And, of course, from the financial point of view, the indie publisher carries the risk, but also takes the benefits. When those royalties start rolling in from Amazon or D2D, no-one is waiting in the wings to take a share of the profits.

Frankly, it sounds like a no-brainer to me. But then, I would say that, wouldn't I? I'm a committed indie publisher, financially secure enough to be able to take a long-term view of the business, and long enough in the tooth not to want to work for anyone else, ever again.

Let's be clear about this. In the same way I said earlier that independent publishing should not be the route of last resort, but a route of choice; I'm also going to say it's not an easy option and it's certainly not one for everyone.

The indie route is appropriate for people who want to work for themselves and be in full control of their writing projects. It's appropriate for people who have at least a minimal understanding of the technical aspects. Not necessarily so they can do it all themselves, but so they have enough knowledge to ensure things are being done correctly.

And even if you decide this is definitely the way you want to go, there are options about how you do it. At the one extreme, there's the full DIY approach. At the other, there's the fully serviced company which will do everything. And in between, there are a whole raft of service providers who will do as much or as little as you specify.

The route you decide to take will depend on a number of things:

- How skilled are you? Are you technologically minded? Do you understand KDP and the other platforms? Do you understand the difference between pdf, Mobi, and html files? Do you have the ability to design your own covers—and unless you understand what makes a professional cover, that's probably a no.

- How much time do you have available? Are you a full-time writer, with the whole day available to split between writing and marketing; or are you a newbie, holding down a day job to pay the mortgage and fitting your writing into the spare corners of your life?

- How much spare money do you have? Are you are just scraping along, barely paying the mortgage or the rent; or are you relatively comfortable financially and able to invest more money? For example, I have a writing buddy who went down the full service route. It was very pricey. But she could afford it and always said, "if I didn't do this, I would probably have a horse!"

- And finally, what would you prefer to be doing? Spending all your time writing and leaving the technical publishing side to someone else? Or do you find that side of things stimulating and fun? I'm in the latter camp, but I realise I'm not necessarily like most other writers in that respect.

Of course, looking at the above points, I realise they're not all complementary. If you are a newbie, fitting writing around the day job, there's a good chance you won't have lots of spare cash to go down the full service route. And that's before you even start thinking about your preferences. But I never said there were any right answers in all this. I'm putting out the questions you need to ask yourself. The way you answer them is up to you and your own circumstances.

Section 2: Technical Aspects Of Ebooks

16. Formatting

Formatting an ebook is, in many ways, much easier than doing the same thing for a paperback. There are no headers or footers to worry about. Page numbers are not needed. One of the great advantages of an ereader is the ability to change the font size at will. This is why adoption of this new technology has reached the elderly more quickly than might necessarily have been expected. It is great for those with poor eyesight, who can increase the size when they need to. And as a side comment, I understand that for people with arthritis, or anyone for whom weight becomes a problem, holding an ereader can be easier than holding a book, especially the larger hardback variety.

There are a number of ways to carry out formatting, and often it's a question of preference and familiarity. It can be done using Word or any other appropriate word processing package. It can be done using Scrivener, which has both standard templates and the ability to customise them yourself; Scrivener is available both in Mac and Windows formats. There are also packages such as Vellum which many people use very successfully, but it's specifically available for Mac Users; and Calibre, which is a free software package, available for all systems.

If you do most of your work in Word, as I do, then formatting an ebook is helped by having a working knowledge of styles and the creation of tables of content. It's much easier to navigate around an ebook if there is a hyperlinked contents list at the front which can be referred to if a reader needs to go back to something they read earlier; in fact, I find myself quite irritated if there is no table of contents and therefore I am unable to find my way to an earlier part of the book when I want to check up on anything.

Within Kindle, the contents list is achieved by using the facility within Word or whichever word processing package you are using to set up the file in the first place. Styles are used to differentiate chapter headings and then these are linked to the contents layout.

With Draft2Digital, the same approach can be taken. It is possible to leave this to the D2D software to do, but I prefer to do it myself so I can make sure it's okay before I start loading the file.

With Smashwords, a different process is involved. Each chapter heading is converted to a bookmark which is then hyperlinked to its place in the table of contents. This is a more manual, and therefore long-winded, way of doing things, but it does allow an additional 'return to contents' button to be placed easily at the end of each chapter.

The whole process of formatting is relatively straightforward and gets much quicker with practice.

However, there are a few wrinkles that tend to come up time and again. And it doesn't help that these will tend to vary depending on which platform is being loaded to and by which method.

One issue that seems to come up quite a lot is the indenting of paragraphs. For fiction, the most popular layout is for the start of each paragraph to be indented, apart from the first one in a chapter or a section i.e. after a double line break. With one of my novels, I found this worked effectively in some chapters, but not in others, particularly in the files produced by D2D, where even the first paragraph was indented. I contacted the help desk at D2D, who quickly came back with an answer. The chapters in which I had a problem were ones where I had a time and place line below the chapter heading and before the main text. Although it was a single line, and I had emboldened it, the software thought it was the first paragraph and hence started indenting on the line below, which was in fact the first paragraph of the text. The problem was quickly solved by inserting a double line return after the time and place line, thus converting my first paragraph into the start of a new section and removing the indentation. Problems like this tend to occur when we're using the sort of sophisticated software these platforms run on, but once solved, it's an issue that should never run again.

While that might seem like too detailed an explanation for a book like this, my purpose was to demonstrate that problems can arise even for the more experienced among us. Often, they have a simple resolution, which the relevant helpdesk should be able to easily provide. I find it helpful to keep a log of this sort of problem when it arises, so I will recognise it if it occurs again with a future book.

17. Selling Via Amazon

17.1 Introduction

Ebooks offered for sale on Amazon are generally loaded via Kindle Direct Publishing (KDP). It is also possible to distribute books loaded via the aggregator sites to Amazon, but why would you bother doing this? There's a simple, straightforward website for doing it directly, and this is the one Amazon would prefer you to use and which therefore will presumably get you the most flexibility and visibility within the system. You need an account with KDP in order to get started, but that's quite straightforward to do and takes just a little while.

17.2 File Formatting And Loading

The final file will be in one of the proprietary Kindle formats .azw; .azw3 or .kfx. However, it can start life as any one of the following formats:

- Doc or docx, which are Word files;

- Html(hypertext markup language), which can be found as a 'save as' option within Word;

- Mobi, which you might already have if you have loaded your book onto D2D or Smashwords;

- Epub (electronic publication) which is the standard format for ebooks on platforms other than Amazon; again, you might already have this if you have loaded your book onto D2D or Smashwords;

- RTF (rich text format) a text format file used in Word;

- TXT, a text formatted file;

- PDF (portable document format), a fixed file which can be found as a 'save as' option within Word; this is particularly useful if your book has illustrations, tables or figures which need to be 'fixed' at a particular position within the text.

A useful tool I have recently started using is Kindle Create. It takes a Word document and formats it on the spot. By a series of check boxes, you can identify the chapter headings and then inspect them for accuracy etc. before uploading onto KDP. This makes it quicker and easier to spot problems with the formatting. Note it is also possible to correct errors once the KDP loading process has begun, but it's much quicker and easier to do it before putting the files online.

17.3 Getting Started

Once you have a book ready for loading, you log in to your Amazon KDP account. There are four tabs across the top: Bookshelf, Reports, Community, and KDP Select. For the moment, we'll concentrate on the first of these.

Bookshelf is your main dashboard. It's where your books will be listed once they are loaded on Amazon. You can see their status (live, pending etc.); the price in your primary territory, and the drop-down menus for a variety of actions you might wish to take, including updating, price changes and promotions. But for the moment, you're just going to select the button for adding an ebook, in the box labelled 'Create a new title'. This takes you to a new part of the site. The process is straightforward and I'm not going to go through it in full detail. I just want to mention a few tips as we go through.

17.4 Details

On the first screen, entitled 'Details' you start with the title. If there is already a print book or an audio book available, make sure the titles are exactly the same. This will ease the process of getting all the formats of the book linked on a single Amazon page. This usually happens within a day or two, but if it doesn't, email Amazon, quoting the ASIN numbers and ask them to link them up.

Once you have put yourself down as author, there's an option to add other names, such as that of the editor or illustrator. I used this to list the person who designed the cover of one of my collections of short stories; but this meant his name kept coming up linked with mine in references to the book, and even came up once in preference to mine. I don't do that anymore.

There are three pieces of information coming up next which always take me by surprise, every time I go through this process—and I've done it so often, you'd think I'd remember. If only someone would write a book giving me an easy guide... Suffice it to say that a bit of preparation before going online would make this part much smoother.

The first is a request for a description of the book. This is the text that will appear on the Amazon page. If you have thought it through and written it in advance, then it's merely a case of cutting and pasting the appropriate section. Make sure there are paragraph breaks at the appropriate points. And for anyone who is familiar with html coding, the usual commands like <i> or <b> can be used to make it look a bit more professional. In the past, if I haven't thought it through in advance, I've written a couple of paragraphs as a page holder to allow me to get on with uploading, meaning to go back and tidy it up later on. But of course, other things get in the way, and sometimes it's been quite a while before I've got around to doing that. How many potential readers will I have scared away with a poor description in the meantime, I wonder?

The next box to be completed is the one for keywords. A keyword is a word or short phrase that a potential reader will type into the Amazon search box. There are all sorts of ways of setting up your lists of keywords, which will be covered in any marketing book dealing with online sales. At this point, you are only allowed to give seven keywords, although there is a way of getting more linked to the book later on.

And finally, you need to specify the categories under which your book will be registered. Amazon allows you to select two, and here, the more specific you can be, the better. If you categorise your book as fiction, you are one of 70,000 books in the Kindle store; there are 50,000 thrillers; but only 6,000 of them are defined as medical thrillers. Those are just some examples I have pulled up today. There are a growing number of books each day. Be specific; search out niche markets; the number of potential readers may be smaller, but the competition will be far less as well.

17.5 Content

On this screen, you start by saying whether you wish to engage DRM or not. DRM stands for Digital Rights Management and is a way of protecting your ebook. If it's invoked, people cannot lend your book to anyone else. Therefore, it would seem like a good tool to use, right? Wrong! It also prevents people from sharing the book across more than one device, and as someone who reads on my early-incarnation Kindle when I'm in bed; on my iPad when travelling; and also shares books across the family account with my husband, I do not want a book that is restricted in that way. And if you are worried about piracy, let me just say nothing stops people who want to steal your ebooks if they are determined to; and anyone indulging in piracy is never going to be a legitimate buyer or reader anyway. So, there's not much point in trying to stop them. Normal practice is therefore not to engage DRM.

The next step is loading the content, and providing your file is in one of the formats described above, this is easy and straightforward.

Once the contents file is loaded, the next step is to load the cover file. We've already looked in an earlier chapter at how important it is to have a professionally designed cover, especially for fiction, where it really is the case that many people judge a book by its cover. To load onto Kindle, the file needs to be a particular size in pixels and also must be in the jpeg format. It's worth remembering that for many people, especially those whose online life is primarily conducted on their smart phones or tablets, the cover will not be seen in high definition or large size. It's therefore important to check it looks good in thumbnail format as well as full size.

And finally on this screen, you have the option of loading your own ISBN number or using a Kindle-generated one. We will go into ISBN numbers fully in a later chapter as it's an important topic over which views vary quite a lot.

Once the contents and the cover have been loaded, it's possible to download, or view online, the finished product. It's important to go through this stage. But it is not necessary to read the whole thing through again. Presumably all the editing and proofreading has been done, and nothing will have happened to change the words within the chapters during the loading process. What you are looking for here is the final layout. Are the page breaks in the right places? Are the chapter headings correctly defined? Are the paragraph indentations correct? It might seem like a tedious process to go through this page by page, but it really is better to discover a problem yourself rather than waiting until readers discover it and possibly start giving you poor reviews as a result.

17.6 Pricing

The final screen is the one that deals with the vital topic of pricing. And Amazon allows you to be relatively flexible in your approach to this. But right from the start you are asked to make the decision on whether or not you want to join KDP Select. We won't go into that again here, but you might like to turn back to the earlier chapter for a discussion on whether going wide or giving exclusivity to Amazon is the right approach for you.

Then you move on to the pricing itself. You start by picking your primary marketplace. The screen initially only shows one territory, which defaults to USA. In order to see all the other available territories, you have to click on the down arrow below, next to the tab for Other Marketplaces. You can set all your prices based on the primary one, or you can amend some or all of them manually.

For the first seven years as an indie publisher, I left my primary marketplace as USA. The main implication was that pricing on the main screen was shown in dollars; I'm not aware of other impacts, and certainly all my payments came into my bank in sterling. However, these days, I change the primary territory to UK before I do anything else.

There are two main options for royalties, depending to some extent on the territory, but primarily based on price. For most territories, there is a minimum and a maximum price range and within this, royalties are paid at 70%. In the UK, the minimum for this is £1.99 and the maximum is £9.99. For most ebooks, and certainly any fiction ones you publish, the maximum is not going to be an issue as you tend to charge much lower than that; however, if you put together a box set, you could well approach the upper limit. The minimum price is always relevant.

Despite the practice of some of the traditional publishers—who seem to work to a rather strange business model and price their ebooks at the same level or above the price of paperbacks, presumably aimed at driving readers towards print books—most ebooks are priced at much lower than the print equivalent. Some people say 50% is the right level, others go for a lower percentage. My paperbacks sell for £8.99 while my full-price ebooks are currently set at £2.99, which is around 33%. At some point, I will experiment with increasing the price, but for the moment, I'm happy at that level. And it brings in 70% royalty, as I said above.

However, there are times when you will want to run special deals, such as when sales are flagging, or as a promotion on earlier books in a series immediately prior to launch of a new one. And at that point, 99p is often the price level chosen; this being the lowest price Amazon will allow your ebooks to be sold at. At this point, the royalties drop to 35%. The money coming to you is a much smaller percentage of a much smaller pot. Reducing price in this way is great for increasing visibility but you should note you need to sell around four times as many books to make the same amount of money. It all depends on your aims at that time.

Additionally, some of the other territories will only pay 70% royalties if your books are enrolled in KDP Select.

Having set the price in your primary territory, you need to look at all the other territories, of which there are currently thirteen. It's possible to merely allow the software to set the price at the equivalent of the primary territory. For a long time, that was what I used to do. I would set the US and UK prices manually and link the remainder to the US price. But then I realised this was a mistake. The market in India or Brazil for example is very different from that in the US or the UK. It makes sense to check out what the market in each territory will bear. And the best way to do that is to do some research. Pick a few books in the genre in which your book is set, and go to the individual websites for each territory, to see at what price they are selling. It's perfectly possible to view each of these sites, just not to purchase through them. Having done this exercise myself, I dropped the prices of my books in India and Brazil to closer to the permitted minimum. In some cases, this means my royalty percentage is halved, but at least I have the chance of making a few sales, whereas at the US equivalent level, I certainly wouldn't see any.

Of course, setting price is an important topic that shouldn't just be based on the level of royalty expected. It depends what your objectives are in offering the book for sale. You might want to use the book as a loss leader, to raise your profile and bring about read-through of other books in your portfolio. This works best if you are writing a series of books.

You might want to sell lots of copies at the best possible profit level, in order to maximise your income. Or you might not want to sell any copies at all; I know of authors who use their books as accessories for their courses or webinars. In fact, for my Business of Writing course, I give away a copy of the paperback version to each delegate.

You might just want to use the book as a present for friends and family. And there are probably other motivations for putting your books out there at a certain price level. Your pricing strategy will be bound up with your motivation.

There is a tool within KDP that can supposedly be employed to help decide on pricing levels. The KDP

Pricing Support tool is said to be in beta testing phase, and it's probably not worth following it relentlessly, but it's a good way of getting an overview of the topic. It examines the historic data for books similar to the one in question and then shows a graph of likely sales versus selling price. As would be expected, there is an indirect correlation between the two. In general, the higher the price, the fewer the copies sold.

But the more interesting graph is that for estimated author's earnings. The potential maximised profit for the author is at the point at which the royalty level switches from 35% to 70%. I've just examined this graph for three of the books in my portfolio, with different selling prices. The graph is identical in each case, which is actually logical if you think about it. It's not so much a tool as a reminder of one of the theories behind the economics of pricing and selling of books.

Having said that, there are other people who believe the market for books is completely inelastic. This means it is much less sensitive to price, and people will buy books whatever level they're priced at. And of course, under this model, the higher the price you set the book at, the more money you will make as the number of sales will be fixed.

As is so often the case, I don't believe the situation is black and white, or that there is any one right answer for this. There are some people, your true fans, who will buy your books at whatever price you sell them, within reason. There is one view that says with 1,000 true fans, you can survive and prosper as an author.

At the other end of the spectrum, there are the people who will wait for the bargains or the one-off sales to buy your books. I must admit that for many authors, I tend to wait until they run a 99p sale before buying their books. But they are always books I want to read anyway, and therefore they do get read at some point, when they reach the top of my To Be Read list.

And there are the people who will only ever download books available for free. Some years ago, perceived wisdom was that making the first book in a series perma-free was a good strategy, as it led to lots of new readers and the increased chance of 'read-through'. In other words, people would so enjoy your first book they would go out and buy the rest of the series. And there are probably a percentage of people who will behave in that way, but it appears to be an ever decreasing number. As we know, the downloading of a book onto an ereader is no guarantee that it will be read; and this is particularly true when the book has been acquired for free.

My own approach is to use the 99p/$0.99 price point every so often; for example for earlier books in a series just prior to launch of a new one; or for the first couple of days after a new one is launched. Or as part of a rebranding exercise. But in general, I price my novels at £2.99/$3.99 and my shorter books at £1.99/$2.99. At least that's my strategy at the moment, but as I move more into paid-for advertising, I may well increase some of the cover prices to test the elasticity theory.

As always, I'm not suggesting there is one right way to approach pricing (or anything else within this crazy industry for that matter). All I'm doing is outlining the questions you need to ask yourselves before making decisions.

17.7 Pushing The Button

Once all the content has been uploaded and all the decisions made, it's time to press the button and let your book go live. That process involves a certain amount of checking and set-up by Amazon and is said to take up to seventy-two hours, but in my experience, it has usually gone through in about twenty-four to thirty-six hours. Maybe for more complex books, it might take longer. In any event, you need to complete your preparations early enough before your launch date, to ensure that your books will be available as soon as they are needed.

But there's one final decision you have to make at this point. Do you press the button so it goes live as soon as it's available; or do you make it available for pre-order? To a great extent, it depends when you finish writing and editing the book and when you are hoping to launch it. For example, I brought out one of my textbooks recently and needed it to coincide with a workshop I was presenting. The book was only ready for publication a few days before the date of the workshop, so there was no point in setting a pre-order period, nor was there any time left to do it, either.

Many people believe having a book up on pre-order is hugely beneficial. It certainly increases the visibility opportunities and allows you to work on the seven-touch principle of marketing - the one that says a potential buyer needs to come across an item on seven different occasions, and preferably in up to seven different places before they will make the decision to purchase. And it certainly helps with the number of sales that appear on launch day. So, it is clear that putting your book on pre-order will be advantageous in some ways. But the question is, will it be beneficial to do it on Amazon?

The Amazon algorithm is a wondrous thing; and as I've said before, if we work out what it does, the chances are they will change it. So, we can't really win. And anything we think today may not be right tomorrow. But here goes:

At the moment, Amazon records a pre-order as a sale on the day it is ordered. It doesn't deliver the book until launch day and it doesn't take the money until the book has been delivered. But the order is registered as a sale when it is made, which could be up to three months in advance of launch day.

One of the things we think we know about Amazon is that the first thirty days after launch are important. That's the time when your book will feature in the hot new releases charts. And that's when, if you are lucky, potential readers will get emails telling them about your new release. And the higher your book is up the rankings, the better the visibility. So, a massive sales surge during the first few days is very beneficial. But the trouble is that if all or most of our potential readers have pre-ordered our book, we won't have that massive surge. Sure, we will see a big upturn on our dashboard; and there will be a spike in our earnings, but there is unlikely to be such a big spike in our performance in the charts. So, if ranking is very important, it might be better not to put the book on pre-order.

I tend to change my view of this issue over time. I have launched a book with no pre-order at all. I have put a book on a thirty-day pre-order; and missed the point where it reached the top ten in its subgenre. I have put it on for the last two days only with a special low price, advertised to my mailing list only, to allow people the opportunity to buy it at a reduced price. Frankly, I'm still not convinced as to which is the correct way to go. But I will continue experimenting until I get what I believe is a good result—even though that may well be a trigger for Amazon to change the algorithm once more!

Incidentally, this above discussion only relates to Amazon. The other platforms register pre-orders as sales both on the day of pre-order and on the day of launch and therefore, the potential spike is fully realised.

And for completeness, I should say there is a school of thought that believes the whole first thirty-day thing is a myth and that ranking on the Amazon charts is irrelevant. So, as for so much in this evolving industry of ours, you make the decision based on what feels best for your own circumstances.

17.8 Conclusion

And that's it for Amazon. There's a lot of information in this chapter, and even so, it's not a full review of everything. There are lots of little bits and pieces that are quite obvious and that you can just work through on the site. I've just tried to give an overview and add some of the tips I've picked up along the way.

If you want more help, there are information points throughout the screens. In addition, I find it useful sometimes to refer to Amazon's own reference book which, despite everything I've said above, is actually available as a perma-free volume: *Building Your Book For Kindle* by Kindle Direct Publishing.

18. Selling Via Draft2Digital

18.1 Introduction

So, having looked in detail at selling your ebooks via Amazon and the Kindle site, we're going to move on to look at your other options, starting with the aggregators and then the individual platforms. And first of all, we're going to talk about D2D. The process for getting a book launched on this site is relatively straightforward and there is a very user-friendly website to work your way around.

As before, you need to start by opening an account. It's a straightforward process and takes just a short while. Once that's done, you are ready to load up your new book and, as you might expect, the process is relatively similar to that for Amazon. In fact, it's going to involve more or less the same steps on every platform; it is the order that's going to be different. There are four screens to work through: detail, layout, preview and publish.

18.2 Detail

For the detail screen you need to have ready the contents file, which can be in:

- Word format (either .doc or .docx);

- an RTF file;

- or a fully formatted epub file.

You also need the title, author and publisher details; description which will appear on the book's landing page at each vendor; keywords (or search terms as they are called here); categories (or BISAC subjects as they are called here—BISAC stands for Book Industry Standards and Communications and can be thought of as similar to the different sections within a bookshop or a library.) You can select up to five categories, although you are warned that some of the platforms will only accept the first one or two. At this point you save your details and move on to the next screen.

18.3 Layout

The first thing you need for the layout screen is the cover image. This is not really intuitive, since the cover might be considered as part of the detail, but that's the way D2D define it. The cover should be in portrait orientation, that is, taller than it's wide. It can be in any of the usual picture formats: JPEG, GIF, TIF, PNG or BMP, but it needs to be formatted in RGB colour mode as that gives the best image result. D2D recommends a resolution of 1600px by 2400px. If you are producing your own covers, then this can be done via one of the standard drawing packages like Canva or Photoshop; if you are using a professional designer—and remember that for fiction, in particular, this is the most advisable route—they will understand all these terms. You just need to make sure they have a full specification. In some cases, it will be sufficient to tell them on which platforms you intend to launch, as chances are they will already know the requirements for each one.

The rest of this screen provides you with a wide range of options which you may or may not need, depending on how much formatting you have already done. D2D will take the most basic of texts, containing the main contents of the book alone, and help you build it up to a fully formatted ebook if that's what you wish.

There are options to prepare

- the introductory pages—title page, copyright information and dedication;

- the promotional pages—also by, new release email notification sign-up, and teaser;

- and biographical pages—about the author, about the publisher.

The only one of these I tend to use is the new release email notification sign-up, as everything else is set up before I upload the file. But if you prefer to do it this way, the option is there.

At this point, there is a helpful table showing the chapters within your book. I'd always wondered why that was necessary, until the day when all that was listed in there was one of my front matter pages and a couple of chapters, alerting me to the fact that I needed to do some work on my styles within the original file, and from then on, I've always checked this table as a matter of course.

18.4 Preview

The third screen is where you can download your book in a variety of file formats—Mobi, epub and pdf—for that important final check before signing off on the design and approving it for publication. However, before you get to that stage, there is yet another decision to make: which style do you want the book to be formatted in? There are a number of families of style available: all-purpose, mystery and thriller, romance, science fiction and fantasy, and non-fiction. Within each one, there are at least two sub-options to choose from. The default style is called 'D2D Simples' and it is located in the All-Purpose family options. I tend to use that one, on the basis that keeping things simple is often the best policy. But there are plenty of other options if you fancy having a play around.

The preview stage may seem a little tedious, but it is important. Once again, remember you are not rereading the content at this point; nothing can have happened to that in this uploading process. You are checking the chapter headings are correct, section breaks are in the right place and so on. And do check all three formats; they are not identical, and it's worth being aware of the differences in case anyone queries one of them further down the line.

18.5 Publication

The final screen is the one for publishing. When you first load your book on the platform, it is not possible to jump forward to this final location without going through the third screen and confirming the file is ready for publication. However, if at a later date you want to amend the pricing, for example at the start or the end of a special offer period, then you can select the fourth screen directly.

In either case, this is the screen both for pricing and for selecting the retailers to whom the books are going to be made available. For pricing, the primary territory is fixed as the United States. Unlike the KDP set-up, you do not have the choice of changing to another territory. The full price range accepted is $0.99 to $39.99, although the recommended range is $2.99 to $9.99.

I explained in an earlier chapter of this book that linking all the territory prices to the primary one is not a good idea, although that is an option here, as it is within KDP. At the very least, your own territory should be fixed at your preferred price, rather than being tied to the vagaries of an exchange rate. The range of specified territories here is wider than in KDP, with each of the Scandinavian countries, Hong Kong, Mexico and Switzerland being added to the list.

The next step is to pick the distribution channels. There are five digital stores on offer: Barnes & Noble, Kobo, Apple Books, Tolino and Amazon. As each can be picked individually, it is possible to select the first four and deselect Amazon if, as one would expect, your book is loaded directly onto that site. You also deselect any of the others which you choose to load directly to.

Next there are four subscription services: Scribd, 24symbols, Playster and Koboplus. You would normally select these, although the last one would be deselected if you are going to load directly on Kobo.

And finally, there are two library services to select: OverDrive and Biblioteca. For these, you have to specify a price, which is recommended to be at least twice the unit sales price. Again, if you are going to load directly on Kobo, you should deselect Overdrive as that is part of the same organisation.

And that's it. Once all the choices have been made and the button is pressed, your book is published. It will be live immediately on the D2D dashboard and will gradually go live on each of the platforms over the next day or so.

18.6 Royalties

It's not possible to give a concise explanation of the royalties picture with D2D as it is a two-stage process. D2D itself charges 15% of net royalties. But what those royalties are depends on the distribution channel in question.

19. Selling Via Smashwords

19.1 Introduction

As I mentioned earlier, Smashwords was the first site to provide an aggregation service and as such, the technology is older and not quite so user-friendly. This in fact becomes evident as soon as you visit the Smashwords website and even more so when you log in and start using it to upload or manage your portfolio. However, it has a wider range of distribution channels than D2D and therefore I find it a useful addition to the portfolio. Unlike Kindle and D2D, there are two ways of working with your books;

one for a new book, and one for when you want to make changes further down the line.

19.2 Reference Material

There is a much tighter set of requirements for preparing a file for loading; however, this is all covered in one of Mark Coker's detailed and informative books, all of which are available for download for free. Ironically, the easiest place to find these books is on Amazon. I did a search for Mark on Smashwords and came up with a series of guides in European languages other than English. I'm sure that's not right, but it's just as easy to find him via Amazon and as there's no money involved, I doubt if he really cares which site we get his books from. For reference, here are the current list of titles:

• *Smashwords Style Guide - How To Format Your Ebooks*

• *Smashwords Book Marketing Guide - How To Market Any Book For Free: 65 Book Marketing Ideas*

• *Secrets To Ebook Publishing Success*

19.3 Adding A New Book To The Portfolio

As always, the first step is to set up an account. Once this has been done, you select the 'Publish' tab. The first thing that faces you is a checklist of things you should not do. And while the second in the list—do not use this screen for adding new versions of an old book—is useful knowledge; and the third in the list— do not upload a book unless you are the author or publisher—should go without saying; the first prohibition—do not go any further until you have consulted and complied with the style guide—is an important point, and one I have already made. If you do try to work with a badly-formatted file—or actually, one that has any formatting in it at all— then the software will chew it up and then spit it back out for you to try again with. It's not called Smashwords for nothing.

Let's assume you've followed all the guidelines and your book is ready for uploading and publishing. There's just a single screen to work through, split into a number of different sections. Let's take them one at a time.

19.4 Title And Synopsis

You will see a number of differences here from the other platforms we've looked at so far. There is a box for title only, with no additional space for a subtitle or a series name. However, as there is an allowance of 250 characters in this box, you can assume it is permissible, or even necessary, to include all the details in this one space.

Next you are asked for not one, but two descriptions, a long one and a short one. The long one, with a limit of 4,000 characters, is the main one used on your Smashwords book page and for most of the retailers. There are certain rules, or should I say prohibitions, relating to upper case words, hyperlinks and prices, which are spelled out on-screen. The shorter description has a limit of 400 characters and a minimum of fifty characters in order to be eligible for the premium catalogue. The same prohibitions, plus a couple of extra ones, apply.

Finally, you must specify the language your book is written in, before moving on to the next section, pricing and sampling.

19.5 Pricing And Sampling

There are three options available: making the book free; allowing the reader the choice of how much they pay; or setting the price (with a minimum of $0.99). There are a few points to make about this. Firstly, the site is a US one and all the prices and transactions are shown in dollars. Secondly, I am not aware of anyone going for the 'pay me what you think it's worth' option, although I suppose someone must, otherwise, why would they leave it there as an option? And thirdly, one great aspect of the site is when you put in a price: it shows you a breakdown of fees and income for:

- non-affiliate sales (those made directly on the Smashwords site);

- affiliate sales (those made through links on affiliate sites);

- and premium catalogue sales (those made through one of the retailers serviced by Smashwords).

The percentage going to the author in each case varies with the net price of the book. For a book priced at $0.99, the percentages are 57%, 47% and 60%; while for a book priced at $3.99, they are 76%, 63% and 60%. As you can see, there are some cases in which authors get a better deal from Smashwords than they do from Amazon or D2D.

There is no facility within the initial set-up to vary the price of the book in other territories. This could be disadvantageous for sales in some of the smaller territories where money is tight, cost of living is low, and a book priced at the equivalent in local currency of a US price, may well be considered as a luxury item. However, you can amend individual prices via your dashboard once the book is published. So make a note to yourself to go in and do this later on.

Sampling refers to the amount of the book you make available for free download to someone who is trying to decide whether they will invest in your book or not. You decide whether this is a facility you want to offer and, if so, specify a percentage. Smashwords recommends 15% for a novel and 30% for short stories. I've always thought the latter was particularly high. Some of my collections are only twelve stories long. To give three or four full stories away for nothing seems a little rash. In deciding whether to enable sampling or not, it often helps to think about your own experience when taking a chance on a new author. I know I certainly use this facility myself if I am unconvinced and I'm sure a lot of other people do too. On the whole, I generally permit sampling, but restrict it to 10% or 15% irrespective of the nature of the book.

19.6 Categorisation

You may remember from previous chapters that categorisation is the equivalent of which section of a physical bookshop your book is displayed in. There is an initial broad category: essay, fiction, non-fiction, play or screenplay. I note poetry doesn't appear at this level. I wonder where it sits?

From here, there are two further levels to pick from. Sometimes the choice is straightforward. For example, my Suzanne Jones series of novels would fall into fiction>thrillers>crime thrillers.

But when we look at this book on independent publishing, it's much more difficult initially to decide where to locate it. It's obviously non-fiction; that's easy. But from the second level list, it could go under business & economics—after all, the series is called The Business of Writing; it could go under Education and Study Guides—since its purpose is to educate its readers and therefore will be used as a study guide; or it could go under publishing. And in fact, with the third category, there is a specific sub-category on self-publishing. So, in this case, I would tend to go for that one.

However, there is a part of me that would prefer it to be considered as a book on business. Which is why it's great to see Smashwords provides the option of selecting a secondary categorisation.

You next have to say whether your book contains adult material; in other words is it something that under-18s should be protected from? And finally, you specify if it is a box set or not. Then it's time to move on once more.

19.7 Tags

The term 'tag' in Smashwords is the equivalent of 'key words' in KDP and 'search terms' in D2D. It's the word or short phrases that potential readers might use to search for books such as yours. And Smashwords is the most generous platform so far in this regard, allowing you up to ten tags per book.

19.8 Ebook Formats

There are two options for file format within Smashwords. If you are loading a suitably unformatted Word document, then the Smashwords software will perform its magic and prepare your book in seven different formats, thus increasing the choice for the reader. These formats are:

- epub;

- Mobi;

- PDF;

- Sony reader (LRF);

- Palm doc (PDB);

- Plain text;

- and HTML for an online reader.

If, on the other hand, you are uploading a ready-formatted epub file, then the software will do no further processing and that will be the only choice available to readers. It's possible to go down this route initially and then upload a Word file later on, but it would seem more sensible to take the more flexible option from the start if at all possible.

19.9 Cover Image

The next step is to upload the cover image, bearing in mind this is going to be an ebook and therefore only the front cover is required. There are a number of technical requirements to be satisfied:

- it must be a jpg or png file format;

- taller than it is wide;

- at least 1,400px wide;

- and a maximum of 20Mb file size.

Remembering this will most usually be seen as a thumbnail, i.e. small scale, it's worth checking the author and title are readable at that scale. And they should match the information provided back in the first set-up section.

We've already talked more than once about the importance of a professional looking cover image, particularly for fiction books. I'm not going to labour that point any more. If you are using a professional cover designer, all issues of sizing and the like will be dealt with by them. But if you are designing the cover yourself, it is possible to amend the sizing within one of the drawing packages. I tend to use a simple one like Paint or, more likely, go back to my designer, the wonderful Berni Stevens, and get her to sort it out for me. But there are more complex options you can use, like Photoshop—a paid-for program—or GIMP—a free program—that will do a much better job, so long as you know what you are doing.

19.10 Select File Of Book To Publish

There's only one thing to do in this section, and that's to select and upload the file for your book. On screen you see a reiteration of the two options: doc file from Word—and it does specify .doc, rather than .docx; or epub—and the implications for the reader of the choice you make, but we've already looked at this in the section above on ebook format and by the time you reach this part of the platform, your decision has already been made. Just select the file and move on.

19.11 Publishing Agreement

This is the inevitable 'agree to our terms of service if you want to play with us' section. It's a necessary part of doing business with Smashwords, and so there's no discussion. You either agree and publish or disagree and walk away. I'm going to assume for the purposes of this chapter that you are taking the former option.

And that's the end of the Publish screen on Smashwords. Now, the more observant readers will have spotted that you've not touched on distribution channels. So far, you have given Smashwords permission to distribute your books everywhere. And that's probably not what you want to do. You have to go to a different screen to sort out the Marketing Channels. You are now going to move to your dashboard.

19.12 Dashboard

This is the screen from which you do everything else in Smashwords apart from publishing a new book, which is the process you've just been through. There are four main sections to the dashboard:

- Sales reporting;

- Metadata management;

- Marketing and distribution tools;

- and book summaries.

The latter is the equivalent of the bookshelf in KDP and My Books in D2D. We're going to focus on the Marketing and Distribution Tools, as this is where you finish off the process of publishing a new book.

19.13 Marketing and Distribution Tools

There is a whole list of options under this tab, mostly relating to marketing and promotion, so I'm going to leave those for the time being and concentrate on the first in the list: Channel Manager.

Smashwords has its own distribution platform via the site that you are working your way around at present. To see what it looks like, you can try typing your name into the search box at the top right-hand corner or the screen. Providing you have already uploaded a book, you will be able to find it here. If you click on the link it takes you to the sales page for that book. And it will contain the cover image you uploaded, the long description, and buy/gifting links. As you are the author, it will also provide download buttons for each of the formats, so you can get copies of your books for free.

However, to be frank, being listed on Smashwords is not a huge benefit, since very few people use it as their primary buying site. It's great as an upload site, but not as great as a sales site. To get the full benefit of Smashwords, you need to be listed in their Premium Catalogue. As we have seen from the pricing discussion earlier, the royalty rates from sales made via the PC are lower than direct sales from Smashwords, but on the other hand, there are likely to be more of the former than the latter.

And Channel Manager is the place where you specify exactly where you want Smashwords to make your book available. There is a huge amount of text on this screen, with explanations of different aspects of distribution, including pre-orders; and links to announcements about specific aspects of the service, or specific distributors, plus explanations of royalty rates from different platforms. You can read this later when you need to know specific details. At the moment, we're going to scroll to the bottom of the screen, past the Premium Catalogue Status Summary which tells you what you've given permission for, until you reach the Distribution Channel Manager, which is where you set those permissions in the first place.

All the possible distribution platforms are listed across the screen and below each one is the choice of 'Distribute' or 'Opt Out'. As always, there's no right answer about the choices you make; it depends on your circumstances and your marketing strategy. However, this is what I do:

I opt out of the platforms I am already reaching via Amazon, via direct platforms, or by D2D; and I allow distribution to the remainder. At time of writing, I have eight channels from which I have opted out; and another seven I have added to my distribution options. These are: Baker & Taylor/Follett; Library Direct; Baker & Taylor Axis 360; cloudLibrary; Gardners Extended Retail; Odilo; and Gardners Library. Most of these are pretty small platforms, but as it costs nothing to distribute to them via Smashwords, why not do this?

19.14 Smashwords Approach To Gifting And Coupons

One of the issues with Amazon in particular is that it's impossible to give free copies away via the system and it's even quite difficult to make a gift of a copy to someone, involving you in payment of the full sales price. With Smashwords, life is a lot simpler.

If you return for a moment to the sales page for your newly published book, you will see not only a buy button, but a gift button too. This allows you to buy a copy of any book, not just your own, and send it to a friend. Actually, the friend doesn't get a copy of the book straight off. They receive an email, informing them of the gift and a link to Smashwords. They have to open an account in order to download the book, but that's a free and quick process.

Of course, giving away copies of other people's books is a great thing to do and probably something that as book lovers—and what writer isn't a book-loving reader too—you have probably been doing for a long time. But if you are giving away your own book, does it make sense to have to pay for it? Of course not. And that's where Smashwords Coupons come in.

A Coupon allows you to provide fans, potential readers or anyone you wish, with the option of a discount which may be between 1% - 75% or 100%. So, you can use coupons to give your book away for free. Of course, there are other ways of doing this and we will talk about it elsewhere in the book.

20. Selling Via Other Aggregators

20.1 Introduction

As I have already said, Smashwords was the first aggregator to the market and it holds a soft spot in many indies' hearts for that reason. Draft2Digital is newer and frankly, easier to use. Many people use a combination of the two. But there are other options.

20.2 PublishDrive

PublishDrive is a relative newcomer, having been set up in 2015. It offers a no-upfront costs model, which is similar to Smashwords and D2D. This means it only makes money if you sell books. There are two charging options: a percentage option, which is more cost-effective when you are just starting out; and a fixed-price monthly subscription service that is more cost-effective when you are making higher sales levels.

The site claims to distribute to more than 400 stores and 240,000 digital libraries. Like the other aggregators, it delivers to all the large players in the market. But it also has a wide geographical spread and publishes in a variety of different languages.

20.3 Other Options

There are a number of more specialised platforms like GumRoad, which is particularly useful if you are selling a digital bundle with your book.

Unbound in the UK and Inkshares in the US are more traditional publishers and provide significant levels of support in terms of editing, marketing and sales, but the crowdfunding element of their business model means you are much more financially tied to the process and have to prove in advance there is a market for your book.

IngramSpark also offers a platform for publishing ebooks, but they are much more often used for Print on Demand books, as we will see later.

21. Selling Via Apple

Ebooks published via Apple are readable on all iOS platforms: Mac, iPhone, and iPads. The necessary software is called iBooks Author and it is free to download. However, it will only work on Apple hardware, so you need either a Mac or an iPad to set them up.

Setting up a Publisher account is relatively straightforward, although it may take several days to conclude. You need to set up iTunes Connect for Apple Books and download iTunes Producer.

Files can be uploaded in a variety of formats:

- pdf;

- text file;

- epub;

- or iBooks.

They are sold only on the Apple Books platform, but you also have the option of free distribution. The platform is available in more than fifty countries.

22. Selling Via Kobo

22.1 Introduction

Publication of ebooks direct to Kobo is done via the Kobo Writing Life site. The process is divided into four steps:

22.2 Setting Up An Author Account

This is very simple and takes just a few minutes. It's particularly easy if you already have an account as a Kobo reader.

You will need to supply your banking details which will be used for payment following sales and also to determine the default currency for your books. Make sure you know the international details for your bank (SWIFT code and IBAN) as well as your specific account number and sort code. You will be able to find these on your bank's website.

22.3 Publishing An Ebook

To publish an ebook, log into the account and select the ebooks tab. You will see the covers of any books already published, and a red button to 'Create a new ebook'. Selecting this button brings up the first of a series of pages, in which you describe the ebook—title and publication date, ISBN, cover file, and synopsis which will be the description seen by potential readers, and categories; load the file itself; confirm the rights and distribution requirements; set up your pricing; and publish. The whole process is quick and easy. Books are reviewed by Kobo before publication, which can take up to forty-eight hours. This Quality Assurance check ensures, for example, that your metadata is correct; or that your title isn't duplicated—if it was previously published via D2D or

Smashwords, have you forgotten to remove it from their distribution system? If your book is declined, there will be an indication of the reason, and it should be relatively quick and easy to make corrections and resubmit.

22.4 Promoting The Ebook

There is a wide range of options for promoting your books once they have been published. These include being featured on the Kobo homepage, appearing in a variety of genre-based listings, taking part in price drops, and being part of the Daily Deal. Costs for these promotions vary depending on the popularity of the genre and demand for spaces. Some are based on a percentage of royalties, while others incur a set fee.

Kobo is an open platform featuring a number of formats. It publishes books in more than 60 languages and can be accessed in more than 190 countries.

23. Selling Via Barnes & Noble

Barnes & Noble may have little or no presence in Europe, but they are a major player in the US market. They have a website, B&N Press, which allows direct production and distribution of ebooks, rather than going via the aggregators. It is simple and quick to use. And once in the system, the books are available to anyone perusing either the B&N website or their Nook devices. There is no requirement for exclusivity and no hidden fees.

The royalties paid on books in the first two price brackets are slightly below that paid by Amazon, but for books between $10 and $19.99, the royalty is significantly higher. So, there could be a particular advantage is selling, for example, box sets on B&N.

There is a useful section on the website with tips and tools for authors, including steps to self-publishing, building your author platform and metadata basics. There is also a whole raft of paid services on offer, delivered via a variety of partnerships. The analytics for tracking sales is very good. And there are a number of promotional opportunities.

24. Pricing

24.1 Introduction

We've already mentioned pricing more than once in earlier chapters. However, it is such an important topic it's worth spelling it out again in its own chapter. That way, anyone who's just dipping in and out of the book, rather than reading it from cover to cover—and hey, whatever suits you best is fine by me—will have all the information in one place, as well as spread throughout the text. When deciding on how to price your ebooks, you have a number of considerations.

24.2 Quantity Versus Quality

You have already seen there are advantages to setting your price above a certain threshold. Using Amazon UK as the example, books priced between £1.99 and £9.99 attract a royalty rate of 70%, whereas anything outside that range only brings in a royalty of 35%.

Some people believe the market for books is inelastic; in other words there is no direct relationship between price and number of units sold. However, whatever your views on how the laws of economics work in this industry, I believe it's safe to assume you will sell more books at a lower price. More people are going to be willing to take a chance on an unknown author at 99p than they are at £2.99 or even £1.99. But will there be a sufficient increase in sales to justify the reduction, from a business point of view? Let's do the maths:

When I sell a copy of *Counterfeit!* on Amazon for £2.99, I make £1.72 in royalties. If I sell the book at 99p, I make just 29p. This means I have to sell six copies at the lower price to make the same as I do at the higher price. Will the price reduction alone be sufficient to get me those extra sales? It's really a case of quantity versus quality of sales.

Of course, it also depends on the purpose of the price reduction. If you're looking to make more money, then it's worth it, from a business point of view, if you know you are going to get six times as many sales. But there are other considerations. Are there other books in the series? Are you therefore using the low price of the first in the series as a loss leader to trigger read-through to the rest of the series, books that are presumably being bought at full price?

Or is it more about visibility than sales in the short term? Are you using it as a way of getting your names to the forefront in a hugely crowded market; or your books on someone's ereader? In which case, it's an investment in marketing and from a business point of view, it's not necessarily about maximising income or turning a profit in the short term.

24.3 Giving It Away For Free

An extension of the low price strategy is to offer your book for free, either as a short-term promotion or permanently. We'll talk about the latter approach next, but first, let's think about a short-term promotion. These can be done formally for five days in a three-month period if our books are on KDP Select, or at any time we wish for our books on the other platforms. It used to be seen as a great way of getting new readers. However, there are so many free books out there these days that, in itself, it's not necessarily going to work. You need some kind of additional promotional tool to bring it to the notice of potential readers, either by:

- BookBub, which is hugely successful, very difficult to get onto, and, depending on the territories chosen, eye-wateringly expensive for new writers;

- one of the other regular newsletters;

- or paid-for or unpaid promotions on social media.

So, in most cases, this not only involves giving your books away but also incurs additional costs.

Once again, whether you decide to do this or not depends on your objectives. If it's just to get your book out on more ereaders, it may work but it won't be particularly good for business. If you are using it as a way of building your email lists or your fan base, then it makes more sense. Although, we need to make sure we do not contravene any regulations, like GDPR (General Data Protection Regulation) in Europe; or more importantly upset our potential readers and turn them against us before they've even read one word.

24.4 Perma-free

And the other aspect of giving it away is perma-free. This pricing strategy, which used to be very popular, is to put the first book in a series online for free, for ever. The logic, as above, is that it will encourage more people to buy books two, three and so on in the series. And for a while, it seemed to work; provided of course the series was worth reading—and there are a few that have fallen at that particular hurdle in my opinion. But once again, there are now so many authors doing this, it doesn't seem to be as successful as it used to be.

An alternative strategy, occasionally seen, is to make book 2 in a series free; presumably this is to encourage readers to buy the first one before reading the second one for nothing.

My rule of thumb is to look at what the market leaders in the field are doing—Mark Dawson, Joanna Penn, Adam Croft, to name but three. They have researched the market thoroughly and their business sense is impeccable. If they are using a particular strategy, then there's a fair chance it works, at least for them, from a business point of view. But what works for one person won't necessarily work for everyone else, so even that piece of advice should be taken with a pinch of salt—or an element of caution.

24.5 Variable Pricing Across Regions

The default approach to pricing within all the platforms, is to link all the other territories to the price in the primary one. But logically, it's not the sensible approach to take. The cost of living is very different for example between the United States and India; or between the United Kingdom and Mexico. Conversely, the cost of living in Japan may be higher than it is in some of the mainland European countries. So, it doesn't make sense to price our books simply by tying them to the price in the primary territory.

We need to take a look at the prices that books in our genre are selling for in each territory. I tend to pick a few of the top traditionally published books and a selection of independently published ones, to show me the range of prices the market will bear in each territory; then I price accordingly. To be honest, sales in other territories, particularly those where English is not a major language, are rarely a large contributor to income in the early stages, but it makes sense to give your books every opportunity to be chosen by potential readers, and setting an appropriate price is one of the key elements of a good marketing mix.

25. Pre-order Facilities

Once again, we're going to discuss in this chapter something that's already been touched upon elsewhere, but for completeness, I'm giving it its own chapter as well.

One feature that's currently available purely for ebooks, is the option to put your book up for pre-order. There are moves on some of the platforms to extend this to print books, so it's likely that this will be available across the board within a fairly short space of time, but for now, we're only talking about ebooks.

For a pre-order to exist, you need to have started to set up your book on KDP or whichever of the platforms you are using. You need the description, keywords and cover image. You don't necessarily need to have the finished book file, although you do need something to be uploaded in order to trigger the system. I tend to use an earlier version of the book, but it's possible to use any dummy file. I know of at least one person who puts up a file that says: "if you are reading this, something has gone wrong with the system—please contact me immediately". But it doesn't really matter what we use since the file will never see the light of day—or at least it shouldn't. The fully formatted, final file—and try saying that with a mouthful of custard—needs to be ready before the pre-order period finishes and the launch day is reached. Amazon specify a three-day period; the other platforms vary.

The purpose of pre-order is to build up anticipation, get people to order the book in advance and therefore ensure a burst of activity on launch day. The book is delivered soon after midnight on the specified date.

And the money is taken from the customer at the same time. But how the sales are treated varies with platform—and that's where your strategy with regard to pre-orders has to be thought through carefully.

On Smashwords, on D2D, and on the direct platforms, the sales are credited not only on the day an order is placed, but also on the day the book is delivered, and the money taken. Hence there is, hopefully, a big spike on launch day. This helps with rankings and with visibility. However, the same is not true for Amazon. Although the delivery of the book and the collection of the money is the same, the crediting of the sales takes place on the day the order is made.

Which means instead of a nice big spike on a single day, you get a long, smooth curve, and the longer the pre-order period, the flatter the curve, even though potentially, the larger the number of pre-orders. This means your rankings for the book begin to kick in from the start of the pre-order period. I have had one case where I reached the top ten in my sub-genre listing; I may even have reached number one and been an Amazon best-seller for all I know; but because I didn't realise at the time the way the system worked, I wasn't monitoring the ranking and I missed the high point!

So, as I said before, the way in which you use pre-orders depends on the strategy you want to employ. I know some authors who set up pre-order in all the other platforms, but not in Amazon. And in fact, some of the platforms will offer a special deal in return for an exclusive pre-order agreement.

Of course, whether or not you decide to use pre-order on some or all the platforms, you need to make sure your book is available for launch day. And as it's not an exact science, that means you have to go live with the file at some point in the thirty-six to forty-eight hours prior to your launch point. The last thing you want to do is get your publicity up and running, turn on all your potential readers—and then realise the book isn't actually available just yet! Better to be a few hours early than a few hours late!

Section 3: Technical Aspects Of Physical Books

26. Print On Demand Versus Consignment Stock

26.1 Introduction

Having spent a long time talking about ebooks which might or might not be the future of this industry, depending on your point of view, we're now going to talk about the more traditional product: the physical book, the print book or the pbook as we're going to call it for shorthand. And we're going to start with a question that exercises many indie authors' minds, especially when you are starting out and finances may be tight. Do you only make your books available via Print on Demand (POD) or do you invest in consignment stock—that's the cardboard boxes of books that so many authors have stored in their spare bedrooms or garages. And if you are using the latter location for storage, you need to make sure it's a dry atmosphere or the pages will curl.

26.2 Print On Demand

Back in the old days, technology required a print run to be of a size large enough to make it financially viable. It depended on the type of book and the price it was going to be sold at. For example, my very first book was a traditionally published management report on the pharmaceutical manufacturing industry. It was a flexi-cover, A4 book of around one hundred pages; it retailed at £595 per copy and was only sold to libraries and university departments around the world. The print run was just 200 (and we sold more than 185 of them, of which I was very proud). For a commercial paperback novel, the economic print run was in the high hundreds, if not thousands.

However, with new technology, the minimum batch size economically produced is one. Which means it's possible to hold no stock at all, but to be able to order as and when, either as the author or the reader, and get your copy the following day in many cases. And that is the approach many authors take.

The advantages of going down this road are significant. There is no need to make an upfront investment in stock; and there is no need to provide storage space. In fact, there is no need to make any investment at all, if that's how you wish to play it. The book can be uploaded for free, and we will look at the different platforms available for this later on; it will be available on Amazon and you can publicise it on your preferred social media platforms; the reader orders their copy, the platform takes their commission, which includes the set-up costs, and you receive the royalties. Simple and cheap. You don't even have to use your own ISBN if you don't want to—although we will look at this topic in more detail in a later chapter—as there are free ones available from the various publishing platforms.

There are some authors who only ever want to produce and sell ebooks. It's not a business model I would choose, but it's certainly one that's proving successful for a number of indies. And for them, setting up their book for POD makes a lot of sense. Hang on, I hear you say; if they're only interested in selling ebooks, why would they even bother with setting up a pbook at all? Well, I once sat in a workshop at Swanwick Writers' Summer School, given by author Peter Jones, and I have never forgotten one piece of advice he gave: even if you have no intention of trying to sell a pbook, set one up. It makes you look more like a 'proper' author on the sales platforms.

After all, it's all about image, isn't it? (Well not 100% image; there's having a good book and an exciting cover, too, but you know what I mean.) And if you want to enter for competitions at any point, a pbook is so much more effective as a selling tool than a Mobi or epub file. So if you don't intend to put any effort into selling pbooks but can see the benefit of having one available for extreme circumstances, then the simplest POD route is the best one to choose.

However, there are some major disadvantages to only going down the POD route. Firstly, the economics of the situation are not as straightforward as upfront investment versus no investment. There are all sorts of opportunities you can create for face-to-face sales. In fact, my launch parties in my home town are always the times when I make the single biggest sales; I never sell fewer than thirty books on that one evening. There are also books fairs; craft fairs; Christmas markets; and best of all, talks to WI, U3A, Probus or other similar organisations. All these occasions give you the opportunity to set up a bookstall. And for that you need stock.

Of course, you can buy them yourself from Amazon or other platforms. But the unit cost is quite high: basically, you are paying full price and the only profit margin is in the royalty you get back from the platform. Hence the option of giving potential discounts to face-to-face buyers is limited. If you are asked to provide a copy for a raffle prize—a common occurrence at fairs and markets—the cost to you of doing this is quite high. There is always the option of buying authors' copies, which are priced at a lower level, but postage has to be paid on these purchases, which pushes the unit cost up once more. I am an Amazon Prime member, which allows me to buy books postage-free. The most cost-effective option for me is often to lower the unit price on my book, purchase the requisite number and then put the price back up. But it's still a costly option, on the basis of unit cost, compared with buying consignment stock.

26.3 Consignment Stock

An alternative to buying all your copies from a POD supplier such as Amazon or IngramSpark is to get copies printed 'on consignment' by a traditional printer. This can be one up the road, which cuts down on delivery charges; an online printer from elsewhere in the country; or even from across the world. I have a friend who gets her beautiful poetry books from India. The finish is impeccable, each copy is individually shrink-wrapped, and the unit cost is comparable to getting it done locally.

There are, of course, disadvantages of going down this route. To start with, there is a cost implication. You have to pay for all your copies up front, and it may be weeks, months or even years before you sell the copies and get your money back. And the smaller the print run, the higher the unit cost. You have to strike a balance between a lower unit cost, which impacts on what you can sell it for; and a lower total cost, which is easier on your bank balance.

And once a print run is done, changes cannot be made without a reprint. If you find a typo or other error after it's printed, you're stuck with those copies.

But on the plus side, the unit cost is usually lower than for a POD operation, which allows flexibility in your sales practices. I have friends who only buy their books via POD and they either sell them at a loss on occasion or fail to be eligible for book sales and the like.

There is a range of opinions about the superior quality of consignment stock over POD. This will vary from person to person, depending on what experience they have had, but it's certainly true that the quality control is likely to be better with a traditional printer. If they make a mistake, they will run it again. There have been numerous examples online of people being disappointed with the quality of POD books when they arrive.

And with a printer, especially one that's just up the road, as mine is, there's a better chance of developing a relationship. If you have a delay or a problem, there's more likely to be a degree of flexibility when you can just pick up the phone and speak to someone you know.

26.4 The Financial Case

Let's look at an example. My first novel, *Gorgito's Ice Rink*, retails at £8.99 on Amazon. And for this, I get £1.41 in royalties. The minimum price I can sell it for is £6.63, for which I get zero royalties. However, I can order them postage free. So, the lowest unit cost I can get them at is £6.63.

I can order a single author copy for £3.98. Those copies will be printed in the UK. Postage ranges from £2.86 with an estimated delivery date of nearly two weeks to £6.34 for delivery the same week. As one of the advantages of being an indie author/publisher is flexibility and speed, let's assume I go for the speedy option. This pushes the unit cost of the book up to over £13. Even the slowest delivery rate takes the cost to nearly £7.

However, if I order consignment stock from my local printer, I can lower the unit cost to below £4, depending on the quantity printed. Hence there is much more flexibility for discounts and giveaways. Okay, so I have to make the investment in advance and decide on a sensible print run size, but from a business point of view, that has to be the most economical solution. And it's all about the business in the long term, isn't it?

27. POD Via Amazon

Amazon is one of the platforms on offer if you get your POD books from a distributor such as IngramSpark, but it's quicker, easier and more cost effective to use Amazon's own platform. And up to summer 2018, selling a pbook book via Amazon meant getting it set up via CreateSpace, which was an Amazon service. But that service has been discontinued and POD books are now set up via Kindle Direct Publishing (KDP), in the same way ebooks are. In some ways this makes life simpler: there is only one dashboard, you can link ebooks and paperbacks together in reports, and all sales are reported in the same place. The main disadvantage appears to be all royalties are now paid sixty days in arrears, whereas CreateSpace payments used to be made thirty days in arrears.

Setting a book up is pretty much the same as for an ebook, although the categories are not identical, which may take a bit of thinking about. The system is free to use, working on royalties only. Files can be uploaded in a variety of formats:

• pdf (recommended);

• doc/docx;

• or rtf.

If you don't have a cover design ready, you can use the online facility or download some templates. Next you decide on the physical properties of the book, in terms of paper type and finished dimensions; set up your pricing; define the distribution channels, and you're done.

28. POD Via IngramSpark

IngramSpark is an offshoot of major corporation Ingram Content Group; it was set up specifically to deal with the needs of independently published authors and has a relatively simplified process as a result. And that is a deliberate use of the word 'relatively'; I mean relative to the presumably much more complex procedure for traditional publishers using Lightening Seed, the other arm of the group. Compared with using Amazon, it's a tad more complex in my experience. The first time I tried to set up a book, using the files from a book already published on Amazon, I had real problems. But, in theory, it is straightforward. And the folks at

IngramSpark are very quick and helpful when it comes to dealing with queries.

If you are using your own ISBN for Amazon and providing all your links are generic—linking back for example to your own website, rather than to your Amazon page—you can use the same content and cover files for both platforms.

Setting up books on IngramSpark is not generally a free service, and you have to pay a charge each time you want to make any changes. It is worth making sure you get everything right first time. However, there are ways around these charges. For example, I am a member of ALLi (the Alliance of Independent Authors) and each year we get a code which gives us a 100% fee waiver. If you have more than a couple of books, you'll probably make back your ALLi annual membership fee in IS savings. There are also other ways of getting these codes, including taking part in NaNoWriMo.

Whereas bookstores are wary of buying from Amazon, which they see, quite rightly, as their major competitor, they have no problem buying from IngramSpark which is part of the company supplying all their traditionally published books anyway. But the cost implications are significant. Book stores demand a minimum of 40% discount and generally also require you to permit returns. Many indies have decided this is an uneconomic prospect and therefore have decided not to comply with the bookstores' requirements.

Another advantage of IngramSpark is they are quicker and cheaper for international sales and deliveries. Many indies who have decided not to use consignment stock get all their own author copies and stock for face-to-face events this way.

29. Distribution Face To Face

29.1 Introduction

Conventional wisdom is that ebooks sell faster and more easily than paperbacks. And for many people, it's true. Which is one of the reasons why some writers only ever set their books up as ebooks. But just think of all the potential opportunities for sales that they are missing out on. In fact, I have always found paperbacks easier to sell and it's only recently that my ebook sales have started to outstrip my physical ones.

29.2 Launch Parties

A launch is like any other party—a time of celebration. It's the opportunity to thank your supporters, do a bit of promotion, get some great photos for future marketing, and hopefully sell some copies as well. It can be as lavish or as simple as you wish. I always hold mine in the local church which is a great performance space; I provide a few bottles of cheap fizz, some tiny cream cakes, and some musical entertainment—usually matching the location of the book. I invite everyone I know, usually get upwards of seventy people there and sell around thirty to forty copies. It's a great way to start the launch activities.

29.3 Book Signings

Often libraries or bookshops will host a book signing, especially if you're willing to provide the money and/or do all the organising yourself. These can be very variable events and often the success depends on how proactively you, the author, talk to people and attract them to your table. And it can be the case that the person organising the event is not there when you arrive and has not communicated well to the rest of the staff. So be prepared to do some last-minute setting up. And don't lose your cool! I once did a signing in the foyer of a library where there had been no publicity, and no-one knew who I was. I smiled at everyone who walked past and, if they didn't walk away fast enough, got them to come and chat to me. I didn't make any sales that day, but I had lots of interesting chats and some people went away to look up my ebooks instead.

29.4 Literary Festivals

It appears every town and village across the land is having a literary festival these days. Well, actually, that's a bit of an exaggeration, but they do seem to be springing up all over the place. Which has to be a good thing, as it's one place guaranteed to bring writers and readers together. Some of the larger, longer established ones are currently closed shops where indies are concerned, although I believe that will gradually change. But many of the smaller ones, and even the newer large ones, will be happy to include you in their programmes. There may be opportunities to present your book via a formal talk, take part in a Q&A session on a particular genre or an aspect of writing, or just be part of an associated book fair. It's definitely worth checking out what's going on in your region over the year. But remember that festival programmes are often fixed months in advance, so be prepared to plan well ahead.

29.5 Conferences

We all need to keep learning, whether it's about our writing or about the process of publishing. These days, there is a huge amount of information available for free online, or for a small amount of money via books like this one. But there is something extra special about going to a conference. It's not about meeting readers, but it's a chance to network with lots of other writers—and doing it face to face is much more effective than sitting at your computer or with your phone communicating via Facebook. Every year, I attend the Writers' Summer School in Swanwick. It takes place in August and is the opportunity to spend a week with 300 like-minded people. It's a great learning exercise, but also great fun. And with a book room on site, there's the opportunity to sell books as well. Not all conferences offer the same facilities; and not all conferences are so welcoming of indies, but if you look around, you're sure to find something appropriate. And even if you don't sell books on the spot, you can give out cards, flyers or bookmarks which may well lead to sales in the future.

29.6 Multi-author Events; Book Fairs

Having said that a conference provides an opportunity for potential sales, even though you are in competition with all the other authors there, I'm not quite so optimistic about book fairs. The good news is that with a book fair, anyone coming through the door is likely to be a reader (or someone who wants help with the book they've just written, but that's another story). But the bad news is there are lots of books on offer in the same location as yours. If I am considering taking part in one of these events, I try to find out the sort of footfall the organisers expect—and this is easier to find with an established event rather than a new one. Then you do the maths: if every person coming through the door buys just one book (and that's quite a stretch target), how many authors will those purchases be spread between, and what is the likelihood of making back your table fee, let alone your petrol, or even making a profit? Of course, that's the pure financial business case for attending one of these events. There are lots of side benefits, like networking with other authors, giving out promotional material that might lead to future sales, and finding new books you might want to read yourself. Okay so that last one's not necessarily good for business, but we're all readers too. However, it's definitely worth having a good look at the business case and the cost benefit analysis before agreeing to take part.

29.7 Craft Fairs

Craft fairs are interesting events. You rarely find authors there, so the good news is there will be less direct competition. But on the other hand, the public will consist of a few readers mixed up among a crowd of people who will never read, at least a book—and will be happy to tell you so. Oh, and that person wanting help publishing their own book will be back there too. Having said that, I've had some great days selling and meeting people at craft fairs—especially around Christmas time when people are buying presents for friends and family. Once again, it's a case of looking at the potential, trying to get some feedback from previous stall holders if possible, and checking out the cost. A book is a low value item, in purely monetary terms. You have to sell a lot of copies to make back, for example, a £50 or £100 table fee in a major venue, whereas a £5 fee in a village hall is much easier to recoup and you may well have more fun at the same time.

29.8 Talks

A variety of organisations, national and local, put on regular, often monthly, meetings for their members and are therefore looking for good speakers. These range for the general ones like the WI, U3A and

Probus, to specific ones like History Groups, Amenity Societies and the like. They will generally let you put up a stall for sales after the main event—and these can result in anything from zero to twenty copies sold at any one time. But make sure you take someone with you to run the stall; you don't want to miss potential sales while you are chatting to one of the audience members, as has happened to me in the past. The WI requires an audition, which can be a bit daunting—I had to face 150 members in a local village hall, and when it's over they discuss you in public—but once you pass, you go into their speakers' book which is circulated across the region. The other organisations tend to be less formal, and it's often a case of doing a trawl through the internet to find contact details for individual groups. I certainly do that for U3A groups. And often people are active members of more than one group, so if you do well in one, there's a good chance of a word of mouth recommendation.

And the other benefit of giving talks is that the organisations in question often pay a fee and/or expenses. So, you are guaranteed to get something out of the event, even if you don't sell many books.

30. Distribution Online

30.1 Introduction

The easiest way to organise distribution of physical books sold online is via one of the main channels: Amazon or IngramSpark. However, there is also a DIY option, which we'll look at later.

30.2 Distribution Via Amazon

This will work both for POD copies and for consignment stock. For POD, the order is placed directly with Amazon by the customer; the book is produced and dispatched by Amazon. There is no involvement by you at this point. The charges from Amazon for this service are quite hefty and the final royalty may well be as little as, or even less than, that for the sale of an ebook.

For consignment stock, you can set up an account as a third party seller. Amazon collects the orders and either fulfils them on your behalf or passes them on for your action, depending on the package you have agreed. The first option is obviously easier for you from a logistical point of view. However, either option involves some hefty charges from Amazon and careful examination of the financial aspects would be necessary before going down this route.

30.3 Distribution Via IngramSpark

Orders come to IngramSpark either directly from customers or via the major wholesalers. Stock is produced and distributed by them. The option of using them to distribute your own consignment stock does not exist.

30.4 Distribution Via Wholesalers

If you register as a publisher with the major wholesalers, orders from libraries or bookshops can come to you for sale of consignment stock. In the UK, for example, the wholesalers are Gardners and Bertrams. Their orders come via an email from Nielsen, the UK ISBN agency. The logistics and costs of packaging and posting is your responsibility, in this case. If, on the other hand, you are registered for POD with IngramSpark, this can be the source of supply: orders go direct to IS and you have no involvement in the distribution process.

30.5 Direct Distribution

There is no reason why you can't sell your books from your own website and distribute them yourself. There is no VAT on physical books; so the sales process is straightforward. Money can be collected via PayPal or a similar banking arrangement and, apart from the minor banking fees, all the money is yours. There is merely the logistics of packaging and posting. At low level of sales this is a viable option, but as your visibility and sales grow, alternative arrangements will be needed.

31. Distribution Via Bookshops

31.1 Introduction

Contrary to what you might have been told, it is not impossible for indie authors to distribute their books via bricks and mortar bookshops. It is, however, quite difficult and from a business point of view, might not be worth the effort. But there is an undeniable thrill to be gained from seeing your books on the shelves alongside other, maybe more well-known, authors. Just be careful that pride doesn't take you down the route of a bad business decision.

There are two types of bookshops: the independents and the chains. The former are easier to work with, as the decision maker will usually be the owner or manager, and it's therefore possible to meet with them face to face. Often there is a willingness to work with local authors, either traditionally published or independent, which means you will be pushing on an open door.

With the chains, the decision is often made at headquarters. And the strategy seems to change with time. On occasion, there is no acceptance of indie authors; at other times, they are positively welcomed. It's really a case of keeping your eyes open for opportunities.

One of the issues I found when starting to work with bookshops was the very real cost in time and petrol involved in travelling to and from them. If a shop is only going to take one or two copies, and only then on a sale or return basis, it's not worth your while visiting them unless they are within walking distance, or are located somewhere that you visit regularly for other reasons.

31.2 Act Like A Publisher

But whichever type of bookshop you are approaching, it's important to remember to wear your publisher's hat, rather than your author's one. And the first step is to make an appointment. This is a business arrangement and it needs to start with a business meeting. If you bounce into the shop and take everyone by surprise, you will not make a favourable impression, especially if you choose a busy time of day, when there are lots of customers wanting to make purchases.

Do your homework first: check out the store to see whether they feature local authors in any way. Consult the website for the manager's name and contact details, or phone and ask. Then send an email requesting a meeting.

Once in front of the decision maker, your time will probably be limited; so use it wisely. Have a professional-looking Advance Information sheet available for each book. These are the one-page documents provided by traditional publishing houses;

you can find examples and templates easily online. I used an article from ALLi (Alliance of Independent Authors) and the associated template to set mine up.

31.3 Pricing

Be prepared to answer the inevitable questions about both wholesale and retail price. It is quite normal for copies in bookshops to be on sale for a higher price than online. This is one of the reasons I never have a price printed on my paperbacks, whether sourced as consignment stock or via POD. There's much more flexibility that way. Bookshops will require a commission on any sales, which is the discount at which you sell the copy to them. The chains may ask for up to 60% and will generally not drop below 40%. Make sure you know your costings well enough to calculate whether you will be making anything on a sale or not. Of course, there may be reasons why you would be willing to accept a small loss on occasion, but this is not a sustainable strategy long-term.

And do make sure the agreement is clear before you leave. I am an intelligent, educated and numerically-literate person. Yet when I first approached a local store about holding a book signing, the manager was talking about 60% and 40% interchangeably in the same conversation and it was only after I left the store I realised I'd agreed he would keep 60% of the sales money and give me 40%, rather than the other way around. That was not a mistake I made twice!

31.4 Returns

Bookshops usually take stock on a sale or return basis. If you are planning to supply books from your own consignment stock, it's easier to control this. I tend to supply just a couple of copies at a time and therefore the risk of high returns or damaged stock is lower. I've only ever had one copy returned damaged, and the shop paid the invoice I sent them. However, if you are supplying your books via IngramSpark, then there is less control. Many authors decide not to allow returns on books purchased by bookshops and set this as a policy with IngramSpark, even though they realise they are less likely to make bookshop sales that way.

31.5 ISBNs

We will talk about ISBNs in more detail in a later chapter, but it's worth pointing out here that having an ISBN is usually a prerequisite for making sales via bricks and mortar bookshops, since they will use the bar code for stock control and for pricing. And even more to the point, they should be your own ISBNs. For stock produced and distributed by IngramSpark, or indeed for consignment stock from your own printer, there is no option but to go down this route. However, if you are producing via Amazon POD, do not be tempted to use one of their free ISBNs. This will make Amazon the Publisher of Record; and few bookshops are willing to stock books produced by their biggest rival.

32. Other Distribution Options

32.1 Local Shops

In addition to traditional bookshops, there are a range of other options you might consider; some are obvious, others less so. And on the grounds that your biggest fans will be closest to home, at least initially, I would suggest you start in your own home town or village. Does the local Post Office, if you are lucky enough to still have such a thing, stock gift items? My books are on display in our local Post Office and it's such a popular place, there's always a queue, which means people are standing looking around them, passing the time. Is there a gift shop? Would they be interested in stocking something by a local person? This is a particularly successful outlet if your books have a local flavour to them. Since my novels are all set in Russia or other far-flung places, this isn't something I've been able to capitalise on yet, but one of the projects I've promised myself I will get around to soon is a series of murder mysteries set in the countryside around where I live.

And don't be afraid to think outside the box. Two of the most successful outlets for the short story collections we published back in 2011 were the counter of a diner just outside town; and next to the till in the local petrol station. Both venues are located on the A38, which is a major route for holiday makers on their way to Cornwall; I'm sure most of the sales went to people stocking up against rainy days in the caravan.

With these one-off outlets, the commission paid to the retailer will often be a question of negotiation; and will usually be less than that expected by a dedicated bookshop whose sole purpose is to make profits from book sales. I have paid commissions of between zero and 35% in the past.

32.2 Craft Shops

There are craft shops in most towns and villages these days, and they will often consider stocking books by local authors. And every tourist attraction in the country has a shop associated with it. They are usually heavily stocked and space is at a premium. But if you can convince them your book will attract customers, then it is worth a try. As with the bookshops, make an appointment with the manager and have your arguments well prepared. Once again, it will be helpful if you can show there is a local connection. Most people who visit a tourist attraction will be looking for souvenirs to take back for themselves or as presents. And if they happen to be keen readers as well, you might well tick all the boxes for them.

Once again, the commission will often be agreed by negotiation, but my experience has been that the owners of craft shops drive harder bargains than other retailers and the rates they expect are often closer to those of the bookshops.

32.3 Libraries

And finally, don't forget the libraries. These days budgets are tight and getting the local branch to buy a copy of your book may be difficult, but it's certainly worth a try as a first step. Here in Devon, there is a central purchasing person, but they work on recommendations from the local staff. In the past, I have contacted our local librarian when I have a book out and she's passed a request back to head office. If direct sales are not possible, then check if there is a Friends of the Library group. These are often fundraising organisations; my local one has purchased copies of my last three novels and donated them to the library. And if all else fails, it's worth considering donating a copy yourself, as it raises your profile. And, who knows, if the borrowing rate is brisk on this one, the library may be more willing to consider buying the next one when it comes out?

32.4 Repeat Purchases

Any marketing person will tell you that selling to an existing customer is often easier than getting a new one. Someone who has already bought and read your book—assuming they enjoyed it, of course—knows the product is good, and is therefore more willing to consider it as a present for the readers in their life. So remember to promote your books as presents at key times of the year such as Christmas or Mother's Day. And since birthdays arrive throughout the year, it might be worth having some sort of regular promotion based on buying a copy for friends or family.

33. ISBNs

33.1 What Is An ISBN?

ISBN stands for International Standard Book Number. It is based on a standard developed by the International Organization for Standardization. The ISBN is a global identifier by which your book is recognised in terms of title, author, publisher and format. There is no legal requirement to allocate an ISBN to your book, but it is used, in association with its bar code, by wholesalers, retailers and libraries for stock control purposes. Additionally, the online publishing platforms will generally not allow you to publish without one.

You need a different ISBN for each format in which your book is produced; and if the book is updated significantly, for each edition. So, if your book is available as a hardback, a paperback, a large print version and an ebook, there will be four different ISBNs to differentiate between each one. The one exception to this is ebooks in Amazon, but we'll come back to that later on.

The ISBN used to consist of ten digits, but since 2007, that number has been increased to thirteen. It specifies the type of material (in this case, a book), the country of publication, the publisher, and the individual book.

The ISBN relates to a book and its publisher. Once allocated it can be used with that particular format and edition of the book wherever it is sold, in whichever country.

33.2 Sourcing Of ISBNs

There are two ways to source an ISBN: you can buy your own or you can use one provided free of charge by the publishing platform, whether that is Amazon, D2D, Smashwords or PublishDrive. There are pros and cons to each route. Let's look at the mechanics first and then return to which route is right for you.

33.3 Buying Your Own ISBNs

Each country has an official agency responsible for supplying ISBNs. For example, in the UK, it is Nielsen; in USA it is Bowker. All agencies are listed on the International ISBN Agency website. There may well be other companies offering ISBNs for sale, but they will have sourced them from the national agency in the first place and it is always better to go direct, as we will discuss in the section on pros and cons.

In some countries, such as Canada, ISBNs are available free of charge. But for most countries, there is a charge, and this can be quite high, depending on how many you purchase. For example, as of May 2019, the cost of a single ISBN in the UK is £89. If you buy ten, you pay £159 (£15.90 each). For 100, the cost is £359 (£3.59 each), and for 1,000, the charge is £959 (£0.96 each). A major publisher, who would use vast numbers of ISBNs, will therefore be paying less than £1 each. The equivalent costs in the US for 1, 10 and 100 are: $125, $295 ($29.5 each) and $575 ($5.75 each) respectively.

The premium price for a single number, if you are only ever planning on publishing one book, is significant. When I first started publishing, I bought a block of ten ISBNs. I have recently bought my second block and this time I went for 100. So my cost per book has dropped considerably.

33.4 Sourcing From The Online Platforms

Amazon does not use ISBNs for ebooks. Instead it uses an ASIN (Amazon Standard Identification Number). If you wish to use one of your own ISBNs for your ebook, you can, but the ASIN will remain the principle identifier on the site. For physical books, Amazon offers a free ISBN as an option.

If you are loading your ebooks via D2D or Smashwords you have the option of using one of their free ISBNs. PublishDrive doesn't use ISBNs, although as with Amazon, you can use your own if you wish. Instead, they have a PUI system (standing for PublishDrive Unique Identifier) which they claim is recognised by most retailers.

If you are publishing via one of the direct platforms such as Kobo or IngramSpark, you need to supply your own ISBN.

33.5 Pros And Cons

The only advantage of using an ISBN supplied by one of the platforms is cost. There is no charge to you; and any dealings with copyright libraries is handled by them too. In the UK, there are six copyright libraries: the British Library is the main one and will request a copy of any book for which an ISBN is registered; but there are also libraries in Edinburgh, Dublin,

Oxford, Cambridge and Aberystwyth. If requested, the publisher has to provide, at their own cost including postage, copies for each location. Thankfully, we are moving to a position where electronic copies will be accepted; but while there is still a possibility they will insist on physical copies, this is a significant cost implication.

However, while copyright always remains with the author in an independent publishing situation, the owner of the ISBN is the publisher. This means if you use a free ISBN from Amazon, for example, then Amazon will be the publisher of registration. And you will have difficulty selling your books through bricks and mortar bookshops if this is the case.

And the other question to consider is what happens to your book(s) if the platform you are using goes out of business, or changes its technology, or has a major technological problem. Are you going to lose your book and all record of its existence?

34. Imprints

One question that indie authors often ponder when starting out is whether they need an imprint or not. And strictly speaking, the answer is no. It's perfectly acceptable to use your own name both as the copyright holder and the publisher in the front matter; and when loading the book onto online platforms.

But having said that, why wouldn't you want to have an imprint? You are not only an author; you are a publisher too. So give yourself a name. I started publishing books in 2011, by which time, I had already been publishing the Chudleigh Phoenix Community Magazine for nearly two years. So it seemed like an obvious move to set up Chudleigh Phoenix Publications as my imprint. I have the name; I have a logo—which I even remember to use occasionally—and that's it. But it helps with credibility when dealing with bookshops and the like. And I sometimes even use my real name, as opposed to Elizabeth Ducie which is a pen name, when I am wearing my publisher's hat.

Depending on which country you are in, you may need to register your imprint and there may be tax implications. In the UK and the US, this is not necessary; you can set up an imprint and still remain self-employed for tax and administrative purposes. But, as always, do take legal advice before deciding what to do.

Section 4: Final Thoughts

35. Audio Books

35.1 Introduction

Audio books (abooks) is a growing market, with people listening to them while on the go or in the car. Originally they were available as tapes. Then, for a time, they were mainly available as physical CDs; and this is still a format used, for example, when driving. But increasingly they are available as downloads, streamed direct to a device without taking any physical form at all. Abooks can be purchased as a standalone product, or as an adjunct to either an ebook or a pbook.

35.2 Producing An Abook

In theory, it is possible to go down the DIY route. The basic requirements are a microphone, recording software and editing software. Plus the ability to read clearly. This approach tends to be more common with non-fiction books where the audience quite likes to hear the author's voice reading out their own work, with all the inflections they intended when writing the piece. And where there is no requirement for differentiation between different characters' voices, or acting skills. But it's a time-consuming activity and it's much harder to get a quality product when it's done by an amateur. It is estimated to take more than six hours to produce one hour of finished product, with the split of recording:editing:quality control being approximately 2:3:1.

On the other hand, there are companies with professional actors as readers which will do the whole thing for you. This will produce a high quality product, but at a price. A novel of 90K words will translate into around ten hours of abook. And at up to £200 per finished hour, the cost of bringing out this product is going to be significant. For many indie authors, it is likely to be a step too far.

A viable alternative being offered by some companies is a 50:50 royalty share, where there is no upfront payment required, but where royalties are split equally for the life of the product (which should be indefinitely) between the author and the production company.

35.3 Abooks Via Online Platforms

In 2009, Amazon established Audible, a digital marketplace for the spoken word, including the distribution of abooks. It contains a site called ACX which allows authors, actors and producers to interact, set up projects and produce finished books. These are then distributed via Audible, Amazon and iTunes. Alternatively, if you have gone down the DIY route, you can upload your book for distribution only.

There are two options for royalty deals: the 50:50 share, as described above, where each partner gets

20% of the selling price, but which requires an exclusivity agreement with ACX; or the Pay for Production fee option in which the producer gets paid an agreed fee when the book is completed, and you, as the author, keep all the royalties.

36. Case Study

36.1 Introduction

In this final chapter, I'm going to talk about the approaches I take to independent publishing and some of the thought processes that have got me to where I am now. This is not a thinly veiled attempt to get you to buy more of my books. That comes at the end of this book in the section entitled Other Books By Elizabeth Ducie. Nor is the intention to say my way is the best one, or that you should necessarily follow my example.

Instead, I want to demonstrate the reverse. There is no one right answer to this strange game in which we are all involved. It really is a case of 'horses for courses'. You need to understand the issues and ask yourself the question: what's right for me, for my books and my circumstances? And then go for it.

36.2 My Diverse Portfolio

Over the past eight years, I have independently published almost twenty titles, and the number of formats is nearly double that. So, it shouldn't be a surprise to hear I take a different approach depending on the type of book and the potential readership. Let's start with a quick review of what I've got out there; it's a bit of an eclectic mix.

There are four novels: one standalone and a series of three thrillers. There are three collections of short pieces, one containing all my own work and two I co-wrote with a friend. Moving on to non-fiction, there is the collection of short business books for authors, of which this is part 4. There is a composite book, made up of parts 1 to 3 of the same series; and a workbook associated with this composite. There is a tiny how-to book on running large barbecue parties. And there are one or two oddments that don't fall into any particular category. We're going to work our way through each type of book in turn.

36.3 Variations Over Time

It's important to understand that what I do today is not what I've always done. Some things made sense when I was starting out, which make no sense today. This might be because my approach to publishing has changed. It might be because my degree of learning is higher. It might be because the technology, and indeed the whole of independent publishing, has evolved and continues to do so.

And by the same token, what I do today is not necessarily what I will do in the future. My requirements change, my priorities change, my portfolio grows. All this may affect how I run my publishing business.

There's an old joke about a man who asks for directions when he loses his way in a maze of country lanes. The wise old farmer he's asking sucks his teeth and says, "well, if I was you, I wouldn't start from here." I've been publishing since 2011; I have a legacy portfolio resulting from the decisions I made as I've gone along. If I was starting out today, I might not do the same as I did in the past. But it is what it is. I have a portfolio of books out there and it's not always possible or sensible to get them all to the same state as the ones I am publishing this year.

While working on the preparation for writing this book, I did an audit of which books were available in which formats; and was surprised to find there were a number of missed opportunities in terms of the various channels in which I have different books listed. Periodically I consider giving the whole backlist a complete overhaul. But that's a huge task and I have to consider the law of diminishing returns. I tend to concentrate on treating new ones in the most up-to-date way and leaving the earlier ones as is.

36.4 *Gorgito's Ice Rink*

Gorgito's Ice Rink (GIR) is a standalone novel set in Russia. Its genre is hard to define, and my elevator speech would normally require us to be travelling from the basement to the penthouse of the Empire State Building but here's the quick version: it's a quest novel with elements of history, romance and timeslip.

I'm starting with this one partly because it was my first novel and, although you're not supposed to have a favourite child, it's the one I'm secretly most proud of. It took eight years to write and publish; and was runner-up in the *Self-Published Book of the Year Awards 2015*, run by Writing Magazine here in the UK. It is also the subject of *A Woman In The Snow*, one of my talks for groups such as WI, U3A and Probus. I sell it face to face at these talks and other events such as book fairs; it also sells to total strangers around the world both as an ebook and a paperback. Five years down the line, it continues to sell. GIR is therefore available in a variety of formats.

36.4.1 Paperbacks

I used my local printer, Hedgerow Print of Crediton, to produce a short run (250) of consignment stock when I launched it in 2014. This was the most cost effective way of getting stock for my launch party; for my talks and other personal appearances; and for copies to give away to friends, beta readers and libraries. I used one of my own ISBNs. Five years down the line, I am on my second print run, although I ordered a smaller quantity (100) this time around. Once these copies are gone, I will probably rely on POD for future supplies.

The POD paperback was produced originally via Createspace, using a CS ISBN. In 2018, Amazon closed down this service and transferred the files to KDP, where the same ISBN is valid. If I was doing it again, I would use my own ISBN, but I haven't done anything about switching it over, as this might have implications for my reviews. I am planning to get it loaded onto the IngramSpark system later this year, in preparation for moving to POD supply only, and will be using my own ISBN for that. At that point, I will consider applying it to the KDP version as well, providing I can protect my reviews while doing so.

I sell the occasional copy to local bookshops. Orders come from Gardners or Bertrams via Nielsen and I fulfil the orders myself. Once I am set up on IngramSpark, orders can be fulfilled directly from there.

36.4.2 Ebooks

At various times over the five years, this book has been exclusive to Amazon via KDP Select or it has been 'wide', using the distribution platforms Smashwords and Draft2Digital. Currently it is registered in KDP Select and I am majoring my promotion on the fact that Kindle Prime members can download it and read it 'for free'. I have always used the respective platform's free ASIN rather than allocating an ISBN. I am considering changing this approach, and applying an ISBN, providing once again that I do not lose any reviews in the process.

36.5 Suzanne Jones Thrillers

There are three titles in this series of thrillers set in the sometimes murky world of international pharmaceuticals: *Counterfeit!*, *Deception!* and *Corruption!*. They were published one year apart, in 2016, 2017 and 2018. Each one has a standalone story within it, but there is an overarching thread that runs through all three volumes, and new readers are always advised to start at the beginning and work through the story. They form the basis of *A Broad Abroad*, another of my talks. Once again, I sell them both face to face and online. The launches of books 2 and 3 both led to an increase in sales of book 1, presumably to new readers.

36.5.1 Paperbacks

Once again, I used Hedgerow Print to produce short runs (250) of consignment stock, using my own ISBN. I am nearly out of book 1 but have plenty of stock of books 2 and 3. As each print run sells out, I will probably swap over to POD for future supplies. This will have implications for both price to the consumer and profitability but will reduce my stock-holding. Of course, if there is a sudden upsurge in demand, I can always reverse that decision with just a couple of weeks' lead-time.

The POD versions were all set up using CreateSpace. For the first two, I used CS ISBNs; for the last one, I used one of my own. They are now transferred to KDP and the transfer was relatively painless. I took the decision to wait until Amazon forced my hand by making the transfer for me; and then just tweaked the details within the dashboard, primarily on the screen dealing with price and territory.

I have no plans to produce a physical box set. However, on occasion I do offer the full set at a reduced price, which has the same effect but without incurring more costs on my side.

36.5.2 Ebooks

This series of books are 'wide'. Amazon is supplied via KDP, using the platform's free ASIN. This is where the majority of my sales have been to date and hence where most of my reviews can be found. The decision to go 'wide' is a strategic, long-term one and I am prepared to swallow low sales until the momentum grows.

The books are supplied to Kobo via the direct platform Kobo Writing Life, using my own ISBN. Other major platforms are supplied via the distribution platform Draft2Digital, and currently using a D2D free ISBN. At some point, I will standardise the files and use my own ISBN (the same one I use on Kobo), but this isn't a priority right now.

I have chosen not to load directly to the Apple platform as I do not have a Mac and it's an extra level of complexity I don't need at the moment, but it's on the To Do list, albeit way down near the bottom.

The next step with this series was to produce an ebook box set, which I did in March 2019. So far it is available via Amazon and Kobo, but eventually, it will be available on all the platforms. This is being marketed as below the cost of the three individual volumes, thus offering a cost effective option for new readers, but still with a realistic profitability for me.

36.6 Collections

This section is a bit of a tale of woe, or at least a demonstration of some of the lessons I learned in the early days. The first book I published was *Life Is Not A Trifling Affair*, a collection of short stories, co-written with friend and fellow-writer, Sharon Cook, which came out in July 2011. We followed it up with a second collection, *Life Is Not A Bed Of Roses*, in November 2012. Publishing these two books was a real learning curve and we made all sorts of mistakes along the way, but it was a wonderful introduction to the industry and stood me in great stead when I started publishing the novels a few years later.

In 2013, I published *Parcels in the Rain and Other Writing*. My first solo independently published book, it is a collection of short stories, flash fiction, travel pieces and childhood memories. It grew out of an exercise I gave myself between finishing the first draft of *Gorgito's Ice Rink* and editing it for publication: to put together a book in a month, polishing a different piece of work from my portfolio each day.

36.6.1 Paperbacks

We used a CreateSpace template to format the first collection and our initial mistake was to choose an unusual size for the book: 15cm wide by 21cm high. It was one of the recommended formats within the software, and is recognised in the US, but is much less common in the UK. This makes it quite difficult for shelving purposes and makes it look slightly less like a 'real book'. However, for consistency, I kept the same format for the second and third collections; only changing to a more 'normal' format when I published the first novel.

We decided right from the start to purchase our own ISBNs. Unfortunately, we left the ordering until the last minute and had to pay premium price for a rapid response from Nielsen. That first batch of ISBNs (10) cost nearly £20 each; which added to the cost of goods sold. I have recently bought a second batch (100) and managed to acquire them for less than 20% of that price.

A common mistake for newbie publishers is to overestimate the sales potential and therefore over-order. And this was our third mistake; or more accurately, my mistake. Both Sharon and my husband, who was the Managing Director of the company, wanted to go for short print runs. I remember banging the table and saying, "if we can't sell at least 1,000 copies of this book, we shouldn't be publishing it!" I got my way—and have been eating my words ever since. Suffice it to say when we lost a couple of hundred copies in a flood in 2012, my immediate reaction was, "thank goodness we don't have to sell all those books!" And ever since, the maximum print run I ever order is 250.

All three books were printed, as always, by Hedgerow Print. I sold them at launch parties; at book fairs and the like; and through local gift shops. These days, I tend to use them for raffle prizes or for other giveaways. Or occasionally, as examples of how not to do things.

None of the collections has ever been set up in POD format. Each book is fewer than 100 pages long and, due to size, the unit cost is relatively low, and the postage appears disproportionately high. Hence, although the paperback is listed on Amazon, it is only available from third parties. At the beginning, we signed up for an account with Amazon, which at the time carried an annual fee of around £30. This allowed us to lodge stock in the Amazon warehouse and sell the copies through them, but in addition to the annual fee, we had to pay postage to the warehouse and give Amazon a 60% discount, which meant we lost money on each copy we sold. We quickly pulled out of that arrangement.

If I was updating this part of the portfolio today, I would get the books set up in KDP for POD. I might not make any sales, but it looks more professional to have all the options available.

36.6.2 Ebooks

When reviewing the portfolio recently, I realised I was missing a trick with these collections. As always, the books are available on Amazon via KDP with an Amazon ASIN. At present, this is the only platform on which they are published, so they are not available wide, but neither are they within KDP Select and therefore I was missing out on possible Page Reads by Amazon Prime members.

This situation arose from the fact that I withdrew all my books, apart from Gorgito's Ice Rink, for KDP Select when I decide to go wide as a long-term strategy, but never got around to launching these older books on the other platforms. Given the low level of promotion these books currently receive, I decided to put them back into KDP Select temporarily until such time as sales on the other platforms are better established. This decision can be revisited each quarter before the renewal date.

There is sufficient material in the three collections to make one full-sized book, or a small box set. But given the age of the books and the other areas on which I am now concentrating, the law of diminishing returns would certainly seem to apply here.

36.7 The Business Of Writing: Shorts

The Business of Writing series started life as a workshop I presented during the annual Writers' Summer School in Swanwick one year and a collection of blog posts I produced around the same time. In 2014, I put all my material into three ebooks: *Business Start-Up*; *Finance Matters*; and *Improving Effectiveness*. They were published at three-monthly intervals and were specifically written with authors in mind. These first editions were written from a UK viewpoint only. In 2018, the second editions were published with all three volumes being updated, and a US perspective added. Each book is between 10K and 20K words long. This book, which is the fourth in the series, was published in 2019. It is at least twice as long as any one of the other three, and therefore is being treated slightly differently.

36.7.1 Paperbacks

Neither of the editions of books 1, 2 and 3 was published in paperback format. As with the collections, the unit price for POD would be completely overshadowed by the post and packaging cost. And the perceived face-to-face market for these books being relatively low, no consignment stock was produced either.

Since this book is longer, POD is a viable option and one that has been taken. However, once again, no consignment stock has been produced.

36.7.2 Ebooks

All four volumes in the series are available on Amazon, via KDP; they are also available on other platforms via Kobo, Draft2Digital and Smashwords. At one point, it was my intention to offer the first in the series on perma-free, in order to encourage purchase of the rest of the series. However, I have now moved away from this approach, although I do use price reductions in promotions from time to time. The next step in the strategy will be to set up a box set, either for books 1 to 3 or 1 to 4.

36.8 The Business Of Writing: Composite

In the previous section, I explained why there are no paperback versions of books 1, 2 or 3 in the series. However, I was very much aware that many people prefer their textbooks to be available in physical form; I certainly tend that way myself. It's often much easier to flick through pages to look something up than to find your way around an ereader.

Plus there was an issue with charts and graphs. There are quite a lot of those in books 1 to 3. But manipulating graphics in an ebook is not that easy and my way around it was to set up all the worked examples and templates on a dedicated website and to include hyperlinks within the ebooks.

But this wasn't ideal; and so the composite version was born. Made up of parts 1, 2 and 3, complete with all the graphics and other supplementary material, *The Business of Writing Parts 1-3* was launched in 2015. A second edition was launched in 2018, following the update of the individual books.

In 2019 a workbook was published, incorporating just worked examples and templates from the book. This is intended as a compromise for anyone who reads the ebooks, but wants a physical book to work through.

36.8.1 Paperbacks

Both editions of the textbook were made available via POD only. They were set up in CreateSpace. Initially, a free CS ISBN was used. But the new edition has its own ISBN and has been transferred into KDP. I use it for my own stock and to supply customers via Amazon.

The workbook was set up after CreateSpace was closed down, and was therefore loaded directly to KDP. It has its own ISBN.

Neither book has been produced as consignment stock, and there is no intention to change this approach at any time in the future. Should there be a demand in the future for physical stock for bookshops, it will be satisfied either via my personal stock or via deliveries from IngramSpark.

36.9 *Sunshine And Sausages*

When I said that *Life is Not A Trifling Affair* was my first independently published book, I wasn't strictly accurate. Before anything else, there was *Sunshine and Sausages*. With the strapline *How To Plan and Run Your Perfect Summer Garden Party*, this is my apprentice piece. It's the one I go to every time I want to try out a new technology.

I first investigated independent publishing back in 2009, although at the time I thought it was a 'playing around' project. I had no idea that ten years later, I would have turned it into a business. At that point, Kindle and KDP were only two years old. I used an obscure piece of software to produce my first ebook. I don't think I ever sold any copies; partly because I had no idea about marketing; and partly because the finished product was an .exe file and no-one was willing to risk putting it on their computer.

My next step was to take these .exe files and pop them on a CD. I designed a pretty label, got some printed and stuck them on the discs. I think I sold about two of those. The rest are sitting looking at me as I type this. Who knows? Maybe they will be worth something one day—but I doubt it.

At that point, Sharon Cook and I started working on our collections and my little apprentice piece was pushed into the background. Until I needed to try out the POD services of Lulu; and the production of ebooks on Amazon and on Smashwords. All of these were initially investigated using *Sunshine and Sausages*. And finally, I had a very short run (fifty) produced by Hedgerow Print, complete with one of my precious ISBNs.

In conclusion, the main lesson from this section has to be when trying a technology out for the first time, it's sometimes helpful to use a file that's not critical, and where the cost of failure is relatively low. I've not used my little apprentice piece for a while now, but as I am about to start experimenting with audio books, it might well be the time to dust it off and use it again.

36.10 Oddments

And finally, there are a collection of real oddments in my portfolio. In each case, the versions that are published will depend on the purpose of publication, the anticipated level of demand, and the potential audience.

36.10.1 *Lavender Chickens*

This was the first anthology produced by Chudleigh Writers' Circle, back in 2010. It was printed by Hedgerow Print, using an ISBN gifted to us by a local publisher and was only ever produced as a paperback. It is sold face to face only, primarily to friends and family, and has no online presence apart from a brief mention on the CWC website.

36.10.2 *Diary For A Day*

This is a collection of pieces produced by Chudleigh Writers' Circle on 23rd April 2011, exhibited during the town's summer festival and then gathered together in book form as part of the social history of the town. It was never intended to be sold, so has not been loaded on Amazon. However, it is available as a free download from Smashwords. It is still viewed several times each month and has been downloaded several hundred times over the years.

36.10.3 *RAMMblings*

This was an anthology arising out of a day spent by members of Chudleigh Writers' Circle in the Royal Albert Memorial Museum (RAMM) in Exeter. It was given one of my ISBNs so it could be put on sale in the museum. A short print run was produced by Hedgerow Print, and once again, sales are primarily to friends and family. It has a slightly larger presence on the CWC website but is not available as an ebook.

36.10.4 *Flashing On The Riviera*

This is a collection of my flash fiction pieces, originally broadcast on the Bea Hutchings show on Riviera FM in Torbay. I produced it as a free gift for my readers to celebrate National Flash Fiction Day in 2016. It isn't available on Amazon but can be downloaded via a variety of other platforms. It has never been produced as a paperback and it is unlikely that will ever happen.

36.10.5 *Chasing Unicorns*

This is a collection of pieces: fiction, non-fiction, poetry and prose, written by members of the Writers' Summer School in Swanwick, in memory of an old friend, and with the purpose of raising money for the hospice in which she spent her final weeks. Hence the purpose was to sell as many copies as possible. It was loaded on Amazon, using KDP and the Amazon ASIN, and on the other platforms using Draft2Digital and their free ISBN. But it was also loaded on CreateSpace with one of my ISBNs; it has since been transferred automatically to KDP. No consignment stock was produced, as most sales are made remotely rather than face to face.

Glossary

Abooks: audio books, which are listened to rather than read. May be available on physical media such as CDs or downloadable via a streaming service.

Advances: Payments made by a publisher to an author is advance of publication. Once the book has been published any advance already paid must be 'earned out' before additional royalties are paid.

Aggregation service: a software platform which manages the distribution of ebooks to a wide range of outlets from a single file upload.

Authorprenuer: an author who is both a writer and a business owner; takes responsibility not only for the writing of, but also for the production, marketing and selling of the product.

Beta readers: an unpaid test reader, representative of author's average reader, who reads and comments on a book or other piece of writing before it is published.

Consignment stock: physical books which have been purchased and paid for by the author in advance of sales; usually sourced from a traditional printer, rather than via POD.

Copy edit: a later stage of editing, to check for accuracy and consistency.

Ebooks: electronic books, read on ereaders, tablets, phones or PCs.

ePub: standard file format for distribution to all platforms other than Amazon.

Exclusivity: an agreement whereby ebooks are sold exclusively on the Amazon store in return for certain promotional and/or financial benefits. Applies to ebooks, and occasionally to abooks. There is no such agreement for pbooks, which may be distributed widely.

html: a file format used as the basis of a web page.

Image colour modes: methods of building a range of colours within an image; may be RGB (red, green, blue) or CMYK (cyan, magenta, yellow and black). Different platforms require different modes to be used.

Indie Publishing /Self-Publishing 1.0: the early days of self-publishing, development of Desk-Top Publishing (DTP), 1990s-2009.

Indie Publishing/Self-Publishing 2.0: from 2009 onward, the age of Amazon, ebooks, ereaders; indie authors maintaining all rights to their work but distribute via a global store.

Indie Publishing/Self-Publishing 3.0: current trend within the industry which puts the author at the centre and the focus on the author's website, which can become a direct sales platform.

jpeg: a standard format for an image file. Other common formats include gif, tif, png and bmp.

Keyword: a word or a short phrase that a potential reader might type into a search box on Amazon or other distribution platform. Also known as a search term (D2D) or a tag (Smashwords).

Kindle format files: files with the extensions *.azw, *.azw3, or *.kfx.

Line edit: an intermediate stage of editing, to focus on creative content, writing style and use of language.

Loss leader: a product which is sold at a loss in order to hook consumers into buying additional products; for example a free book, a specially-written short-story, an introductory module to a longer training course.

Metadata: all the elements that go towards defining a book; title, author, ISBN, keywords etc. Everything that helps o identify your book and raise its visibility.

mobi: a file format used to deliver ebooks to Kindles and devices running the Kindle app.

Pbooks: physical books, whether paperback or hard back. Also known as paper books or print books.

Permafree: a book that is distributed at no charge on a long-term (permanent) basis, rather than as a short-term special promotion. Used as a hook to draw readers to other books in the series or the portfolio.

pdf: a file format developed to transmit electronic documents in a fixed layout.

Platform: The combination of activities which enhance a writer's ability to sell books; the visibility of the writer to the reading public.

Read-through: the degree to which a reader, having read the first in a series, which may have been given away for free or heavily advertised, will buy additional books in the series, thus increasing income at no additional cost.

Social media: platforms such as FaceBook, Twitter, Instagram, LinkedIn or Pinterest, used to reach large numbers of people who may or may not be personally known to the account holder.

Structural edit: an early stage of editing, to focus on the development of the storyline and the structure of the piece.

Traditional publishing: where an author uses an agent to place a book with a publisher; or latterly where an author works directly with a smaller publisher. Responsibility for all costs and much of the decision making rests with the publisher.

Wide (Going Wide): making ebooks available for sale on a wide range of stores; the opposite of Amazon's exclusivity agreement (see above).

Word format files: files with the extensions *.doc, *.docx, or *.rtf.

References

Adam Croft/Indie Author Mindset:
https://indieauthormindset.com/

Alliance of Independent Authors:
https://www.allianceindependentauthors.org/

Amazon (UK): https://www.amazon.co.uk;
Amazon (USA): https://www.amazon.com/; **sites
for other countries** may be found by replacing .co.uk
or .com with the appropriate country code

Apple iBooks: https://www.apple.com/uk/ibooks-
author/

Audible: https://www.audible.co.uk/

Barnes&Noble/B&N Press:
https://press.barnesandnoble.com/

Berni Stevens:
http://www.bernistevensdesign.com/

BookBub Partners: https://partners.bookbub.com/

BookFunnel: https://bookfunnel.com/

Bowker: http://www.bowker.com/

Building Your Book For Kindle by Kindle Direct Publishing: https://www.amazon.co.uk/Building-Your-Kindle-Direct-Publishing-ebook/dp/B007URVZJ6/

Calibre: https://calibre-ebook.com/

Canva: https://www.canva.com/

Chudleigh Phoenix Community Magazine: https://chudleighphoenix.co.uk/

Draft2Digital: https://www.draft2digital.com/

GIMP: https://www.gimp.org/

GumRoad: https://gumroad.com/

Hedgerow Print: https://www.hedgerowprint.co.uk/home

Ingram Content Group: https://www.ingramcontent.com/

IngramSpark: https://www.ingramspark.com/

Inkshares: https://www.inkshares.com/

International ISBN Agency: https://www.isbn-international.org/

Joanna Penn/The Creative Penn: https://www.thecreativepenn.com/

Kobo/Kobo Writing Life: https://www.kobo.com/gb/en/p/writinglife

Mark Dawson/Self-Publishing Formula: https://selfpublishingformula.com/

National Novel Writing Month: https://www.nanowrimo.org/

Nielsen ISBN Store: https://www.nielsenisbnstore.com/

PayPal: https://www.paypal.com

Peter Jones: https://peterjonesselfhelpbooks.wordpress.com/

Photoshop: https://www.adobe.com

PublishDrive: https://www.publishdrive.com/

Romantic Novelists Association: https://romanticnovelistsassociation.org/

Scrivener: https://www.literatureandlatte.com/scrivener/overview

Secrets To Ebook Publishing Success: https://www.amazon.co.uk/Secrets-Publishing-Success-Smashwords-Guides-ebook/dp/B007P8H80A/

Smashwords: https://www.smashwords.com/

Smashwords Style Guide - How To Format Your Ebooks: https://www.amazon.co.uk/Smashwords-Style-Guide-Format-Guides-ebook/dp/B004XWJ7UK/

Smashwords Book Marketing Guide - How To Market Any Book For Free: 65 Book Marketing Ideas: https://www.amazon.co.uk/Smashwords-

Book-Marketing-Guide-Market-
ebook/dp/B004XR57PE/

Society of Authors, The:
https://www.societyofauthors.org/

Swanwick Writers' Summer School:
https://www.swanwickwritersschool.org.uk/

Unbound: https://unbound.com/

Vellum: https://vellum.pub/

Wordpress: https://wordpress.org/

Writing Magazine: https://www.writers-
online.co.uk/

Enjoyed This Book?

Reviews and recommendations are very important to an author and help contribute to a book's success. If you have enjoyed *The Business of Writing Part 4 Independent Publishing* please recommend it to your writer friends and colleagues or, better still, buy them a copy for their birthday or Christmas. And please consider posting a review on your preferred review site

.

About Elizabeth Ducie

Elizabeth Ducie has an MBA (Masters in Business Administration) from the School of Management at Cranfield University, under her married name of McCormick, and a wealth of experience in different types of businesses. For more than twenty years, she ran a technical consultancy, a limited company which she set up and co-owned with her husband, Michael. For part of that time, she was also employed by a large multi-national corporation. She has worked with a wide range of businesses and other organisations across the world. She is now self-employed as a full-time author and publisher.

Elizabeth is an experienced trainer and presenter who has been writing training manuals and courses throughout her career. Her workshops on *The Business of Writing* are a regular feature at the annual Writers' Summer School in Swanwick, Derbyshire.

Elizabeth has written throughout her life. She was initially published at the age of fourteen, when she won a competition in the local newspaper. Her technical writing runs to millions of words in reports, manuals and courses, plus articles for scientific journals and several text books. These days she concentrates on fiction and creative non-fiction. In addition to *The Business of Writing*, she has published three collections of short stories and four novels

Other Books By Elizabeth Ducie

The Business Of Writing

Part 1 Business Start-Up (ebook)

Part 2 Finance Matters (ebook)

Part 3 Improving Effectiveness (ebook)

Parts 1-3 (paperback)

Parts 1-3 workbook (paperback)

Novels

Corruption!

Deception!

Counterfeit!

Gorgito's Ice Rink

Miscellaneous

Sunshine and Sausages

Parcels in the Rain and Other Writing

Written With Sharon Cook

Life is Not a Trifling Affair

Life is Not a Bed of Roses

To contact Elizabeth or to find out more about
Chudleigh Phoenix Publications:

elizabeth@elizabethducie.co.uk;

www.elizabethducie.co.uk;

Printed in Great Britain
by Amazon